Android Programming Guide

Android App Development

Learn In A Day!

2nd Edition

By Os Swift

Contents

Introduction

Right now, Android app development is in huge demand and the result is that the platform with the funny green robot is turning into one of the major options, instead of taking second place to Apple's iOS.

There are more than a billion Android devices activated today, making it an exciting place to turn your dream into an app; an app that can help you to organize, communicate, educate, entertain, or anything else you can possibly think of. There really are no limits when it comes to designing an app for the Android platform and turning it into reality is not much more difficult than coming up with the idea in the first place!

If you want a few more reasons why you should choose Android, try these on for size:

- Android has, at the time of writing, the biggest market share of smartphones and tablets in the world.
- Android has a policy on app provisioning and submission that s way more open that iOS. This means that, once your app is complete – and I will be walking you through your first one in this book – you can get it out into the market and onto people's devices immediately
- It isn't all about the iPhone anymore. There are so many more devices on the market these days and

Android is installed on a very large number of them. That makes it one of the most important platforms for you to begin your journey on.

So, if you have been toying with the idea of creating an app for Android, this is the book for you. I am going to tell you exactly how to get started and show you how to create your very first app.

Chapter 1: Android Overview

Android is an operating system for mobiles developed by the Google Corporation. Android is a Linux kernel based operating system. The user interface of the android operating system is direct manipulation based. This is primarily designed for touchscreen smartphones and tablets. Apart from these, android can also be used for wristwatches (Android wear), televisions (Android TV) and cars (Android auto). The operating system makes use of the touch inputs which loosely correspond to the real world actions, like pinching, tapping, swiping and reverse pinching for manipulating the virtual keyboard and the on-screen objects. This is not all, android is also used with digital cameras, gaming consoles, personal computers and a few other electronics. Of all the operating systems in the market, Android holds the largest installed base.

Android is a customizable, ready-made and low-cost operating system that can be used with high-tech devices and for this reason it is popular with technology companies.

Android is open source and this encouraged a huge community of enthusiasts and developers to use its code for developing community driven projects with which they can add additional features for advanced users. They can also install android on devices that run on other OS.

Features of Android

Android is a flexible and powerful OS that is competing with the Apple iOS and other such operating systems like Windows 8.1. Few of its features are given below.

Feature	Description
Beautiful UI	The basic screening of the android operating system provides an intuitive and beautiful user interface.
Connectivity	CDMA, UMTS, GSM/EDGE, LTE, EV-DO, Wi-Fi, NFC, Bluetooth, IDEN and WiMAX.
Storage	Android uses a lightweight relational database called the SQLite for storing data.
Media support	H.263, H.264, AMR, AMR-WB, MPEG-4 SP, AAC 5.1, AAC, HE-AAC, MIDI, GIF, WAV, Ogg Vorbis, PNG, MP3, BMP and JPEG
Messaging	MMS and SMS

Web browser	The web browser of android is based on the WebKit layout engine and is coupled with the V8 JavaScript engine of chrome, supporting the CSS3 and HTML5. The WebKit layout engine is an open source engine.
Multi-touch	Multi touch is natively supported by android and it was available initially with the mobiles like HTC hero.
Multi-tasking	Users can navigate from one application to another application and multiple applications can be run simultaneously at the same time.
Resizable widgets	The default widgets and the widgets you download can be resized. They can be made smaller to save space or they can be expanded to show more content.
Multi-Language	Single and bidirectional text is supported by android.
GCM	Using the Google Cloud messaging, developers can send short messages to the android users. This doesn't need a proprietary sink solution.
Wi-Fi Direct	Wi-Fi Direct is a technology that lets applications to pair directly enabling a high-speed peer to peer connection after discovering.

Android Beam	Android Beam is based on the near field communication technology. Users can share data instantly just by touching the two devices which has NFC enabled on them.

After developing an android application, it can be packaged and sold easily either through the Google play store, Mobango, Amazon Appstore, slide ME, Opera mobile store or F-droid.

Android is running currently on billions of devices that include tablets, mobile phones, TVs etc. It is used in almost 200 countries around the globe. Android is the largest mobile platform base and it is yet growing fast. According to the Google Corporation, more than 1,000,000 new android devices are activated daily.

What is API level?

API Level is the number given to the framework API revision for its unique identification. The android platform offers these.

Platform Version	API Level	VERSION_CODE	
Android	22	LOLLIPOP_MR1	

5.1			
Android 5.0	21	LOLLIPOP	
Android 4.4W	20	KITKAT_WATCH	KitKat for Wearables Only
Android 4.4	19	KITKAT	
Android 4.3	18	JELLY_BEAN_MR2	
Android 4.2, 4.2.2	17	JELLY_BEAN_MR1	
Android 4.1, 4.1.1	16	JELLY_BEAN	
Android 4.0.3, 4.0.4	15	ICE_CREAM_SANDWICH_MR1	
Android 4.0, 4.0.1, 4.0.2	14	ICE_CREAM_SANDWICH	

Android 3.2	13	HONEYCOMB_MR2	
Android 3.1.x	12	HONEYCOMB_MR1	
Android 3.0.x	11	HONEYCOMB	
Android 2.3.4 Android 2.3.3	10	GINGERBREAD_MR1	
Android 2.3.2 Android 2.3.1 Android 2.3	9	GINGERBREAD	
Android 2.2.x	8	FROYO	
Android 2.1.x	7	ECLAIR_MR1	
Android 2.0.1	6	ECLAIR_0_1	

Android 2.0	5	ECLAIR
Android 1.6	4	DONUT
Android 1.5	3	CUPCAKE
Android 1.1	2	BASE_1_1
Android 1.0	1	BASE

Interface

The default android user interface is based on touch inputs, direct manipulation actions like pinching, swiping, and reverse pinching for manipulating the on-screen objects and virtual keyboard. Android is designed in such a way that the response to the user's input is immediate, along with a smooth touch interface. The android operating system also uses the vibration feature of the device for providing the user with haptic feedback. Internal hardware like proximity sensors, gyroscopes and accelerometers can be used by the applications. This internal hardware can be used for adjusting the screen orientation using the gyroscope; Control remote controlled using the accelerometer etc. Home screen can be made up of different pages, which the user can select and add. They can swipe through the home screens. Users can add additional widgets or application shortcuts on different home screens matching their taste.

Memory management

Most of the android devices or all of the android mobile devices run on battery. So, for increasing the battery life, the RAM should consume as less power as possible as they are not like the desktop devices which can have a continuous power supply. Whenever an android app is minimized or when it is no longer in use, it will be suspended in the memory automatically. Technically speaking, these applications will be still open but they cannot consume the system resources. They will wait in the background till the user calls for them again. This gives the users a benefit where they need not close the application and start everything from the beginning. The second benefit of this is that the applications running in the background do not consume system resources unnecessarily.

Android is very good with managing applications. If the memory is low, android will simply terminate the processes and applications that are inactive. It will perform this in the reverse order of their last usage; the oldest applications will be closed first. All of these processes will be running in the background and the user cannot see it. This leaves the user the pain of managing the apps as Android automatically terminates the applications.

Open-source community

The android community can be called as the most active community where many enthusiasts and android developers use the source code of the Android Open Source Project, AOSP. They use it for developing and distributing their own versions of the modified operating system. The releases made in the community are often faster compared to the official releases. The updates that are released by the developers are not extensively tested like the official manufacturer's release versions. There are many developers who release their updates for devices that are no longer supported by the manufacturers.

Security and privacy

Android applications run in a sandbox, an isolated area of the system that does not have access to the rest of the system's resources, unless the user explicitly grants access permissions when the application is installed. Before installing an application, Play Store displays all required permissions: a game may need to enable vibration or save data to an SD card, for example, but should not need to read SMS messages or access the phonebook. After reviewing these permissions, the user can choose to accept or refuse them, installing the application only if they accept. The sandboxing and permissions system lessens the impact of vulnerabilities and bugs in applications, but developer confusion and limited documentation has resulted in applications routinely requesting unnecessary permissions, reducing its effectiveness.

The advantages of the android are many and the android operating system is used on more than a billion tablets and smartphones.

Supports 2D, 3D graphics

The android OS supports platforms like 2D and 3D. Earlier, we only used to watch videos or play games in 2D. The situation is different now and many applications are using the 3D format for better user experience. The android operating system supports 3D format along with 2D format, providing the users with a better experience when using gaming and video applications.

Supports Multiple Languages

Android supports many languages. Almost all of the majorly used languages are supported and the list goes more than 100. With this feature android can easily adapt

We can say all famous languages about more than 100. By using this feature it is easy to adapt to different languages. Earlier in the feature phones English is to be the only language in the mobile devices.

Java Support

Android supports Java enabling the Java developers to add additional features. The operating can be deployed as it supports Java

Faster Web Browser

Android operating system comes with preloaded web browser that can be used for surfing the Internet without complexity. It is similar to that of a computer. Multimedia on the web pages will be loaded easily, resulting in the faster web browsing.

It Supports MP4, 3GP, MPEG4, MIDI

Different video formats are supported by the Android OS. In fact, almost all of the video formats are supported. This will rule out the pain of converting the video into a computable format. Android also supports a wide range of audio formats.

Additional Hardware Support

A new hardware can be connected easily with devices running on android. A device can be connected internally, providing we use it with additional features. Android extends its support to a wide range of hardware devices.

Video Calling

Video calls can be made with faster data connections. The new generation networks and bandwidth can be taken advantage of using the android operating system.

Open Source Framework

It makes users to make their own applications and to make changes required for them. Enthusiasts can make Android more powerful and useful by developing themselves. As it is an open source operating system, we can use it easily and without cost in the equipment.

Uses of Tools are Very Simple

In android, a single button can be used for multiple purposes and it can perform more tasks than for which it is assigned to. For instance, the volume button can be used for capturing a photo just by changing a simple algorithm.

Availability of Apps

There are millions of applications available free of cost in the Google play store. Users have the freedom of installing applications from third-party publishers.

Great Social Networking Integration

Multiple social networking websites can be integrated and their features can be enhanced. This will make it easy for a user to check his social networking accounts easily. By using the user enabled development, users can customize the features and applications.

Better Notification System

Users can directly check the important notifications from the dashboard, making work easier. Earlier, we had to open the application and refresh it for checking updates.

Updated User Interface Design

Interfacing, the user to device interfacing can be updated in the android operating system. The addition of touchscreen can be considered as a revolution and it changed the way people using mobiles. Features like typing and can be effectively performed on a device running on the android operating system.

At a Time Applications

Android allows users to run multiple applications at the same time. This will help the users in saving their efforts and time.

Low Chance of Crashing

The android operating system is smooth and it is very easy to operate. The chances of crashing are less.

Stability

The security and stability of the android OS is superior compared to the other mobile operating systems. The android operating system is based on the Linux kernel and it is the reason for its stability. Any operation that is performed will go into the command mode. If there are any security threats detected, it will go into the basic mode and stores to other applications like cloud computing and it will crash the data stored on the device.

You can change your settings quicker

The settings can be changed quickly. By using different tasks and apps, we can use the android OS.

More options with limited budget

Compared to other operating systems, android is cheaper and it gives a better performance at the same time. It is open framework and open source.

Android provides support for larger resolutions and screens.

Users can enjoy clear and bright formats with android's support for different screen sizes for enhanced resolutions and applications.

Copy paste functionalities throughout the system

Earlier, we were only allowed to copy and paste in a single application. Developers thought of changing this and planned to make the whole phone operating as a computer based OS. For this, the android OS came with the copy and paste option throughout the system. Editing is made simpler with this.

Redesigned Multi Touch Software Keyboard

Android gave users more freedom by providing them redesigned keyboards like Google keyboard, different types of qwerty keyboards etc,. There are a number of smart keyboards available now that made vast changes in the way users type. Typing has been made easy by using the dictionary that suggests users with words and the AutoCorrect option corrects misspelled words. Additional features like drag and detect has brought a revolution in the area of mobile typing.

Audio, Graphical and Input Enhancements for Game Developers

A number of changes were made by android in the multimedia used for the mobile devices. Using different audio enhancements enhances the audio quality of the device.

Improved Power Management and Application Control

The android application control and power management only allows currently running application to use the RAM memory and power. All the other applications will run in the background and will wait for the user to use them. After the user switching to a different application, the system will allocate power and memory using this method. The system memory and power can be saved using the improved power management and application control. The enhanced application control now supports multiple cameras.

Chapter 2: Android Architecture

Before going deep into the android development, firstly you should know the basic internal architecture. The application framework can be understood easily if you know how things work and how they are arranged. Applications can be designed in a better way by knowing these two things. Since the android operating system is based on the Linux OS, it is very much similar to the Linux operating system. The architecture of android is illustrated in the following figure. OEMs provide the software stocks that are above the hardware. The applications are the topmost layer.

Android Architecture

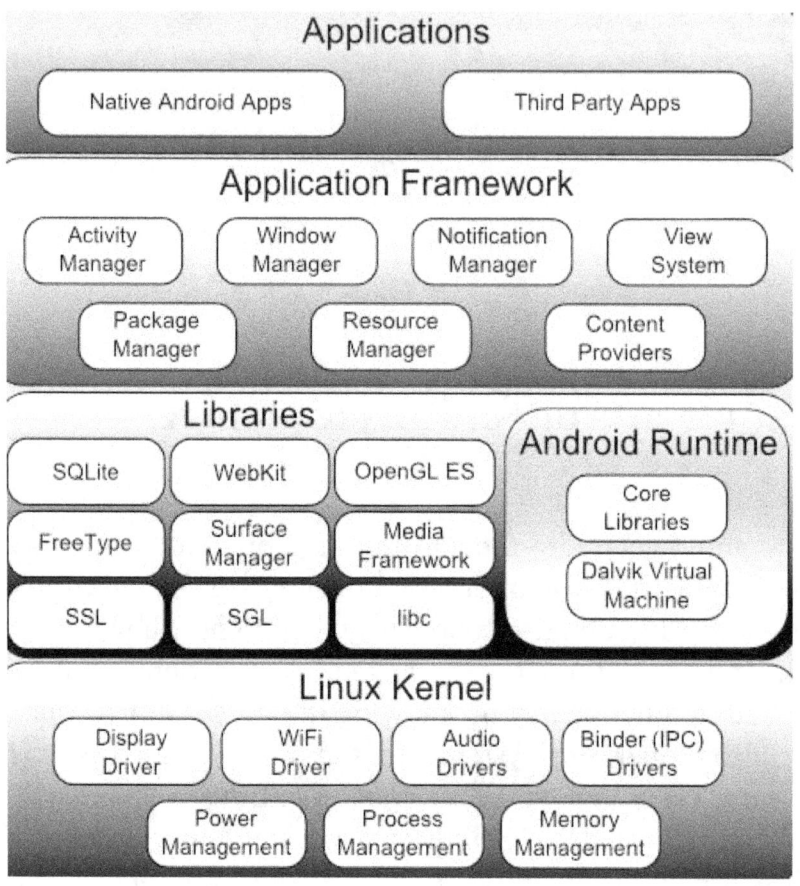

Basic Applications

For instance, four basic apps like App 1, App 2, App 3 and App 4are depicted like any android user interface. Applications like camera, music player, Application for making calls and so on are some of the apps. These applications can be from providers other than Google, Google doesn't necessarily provide these apps. By using the Google play store, you can develop an application and can place it there, making it available for all. You can develop to the applications in Java and install them directly without needing to integrate with the android operating system.

Application Framework

The application framework is used for developing applications. Developers for developing applications use the framework. The framework offers a number of interfaces and the developers of different standards use these interfaces. By using the frameworks you need not code every basic task. There are different entities in the framework and they are as follows.

Activity Manager

The activity manager is responsible for managing the activities that control the app lifecycle and it has many states. The applications may consist of multiple activities that include their own application life cycle. Whenever an app is launched, one main activity will be started. A window is usually given to every activity in an app that has got its own user interface and layout.

Notification Manager

The notification manager enables the apps to display custom alerts.

Views

Views are used for creating layouts that includes components like buttons, lists and the grids.

Resource Managers

The applications require external resources like external strings which are managed by resource manager, graphics etc,. The resource managers allot these resources in a standardized way.

Content Provider

Data is shared by the applications whenever it is required. Applications sometimes may need the data from other a. The calling app will require access to the contact list of the user. The content provider will allow the access to the data of other applications.

Libraries

All the native libraries of android will be present in this layer. These libraries are written in C and C++. The capabilities of these libraries are similar to the application layer present on the topmost layer of the Linux kernel. Some of the major native libraries consist of the following.

- Surface Manager: The compositing window in manager and display.

- Media framework: this framework consists of the codecs and audio, video formats. It also includes their recording and playback.
- System C Libraries: these basic C libraries are targeted for the embedded devices or ARM.
- OpenGL ES Libraries: 3D and 2D graphics.
- SQLite: SQLite is a database engine.

Android Libraries

The Java libraries that are specific to the android development are present in this category. The application framework libraries are an example to this library. The application framework library is an additional package to other libraries that help in graphics drawing, user interface building and database access. Some of the core android libraries and they summaries are given below.

- android.app – Library is considered as the cornerstone for all the android applications and it also provides the required access to the application models.
- android.content – Publishing, content access and messaging in between apps and their components are supported by this library.
- android.database – This library will allow the access of the data that is published by content providers. This library also includes the database management classes of SQLite
- android.opengl – this library is the Java interface today 3-D graphics rendering API, OpenGL ES.
- android.os – the access to the standard OS services like system services, messages and interposes

communication are provided to the applications by this library.

- android.text – Text can be rendered and manipulated using this library on a display device.
- android.view – the application user interface building blocks are provided by this library. These building blocks are the fundamental building blocks.
- android.widget – this library is a collection of UI components that are prebuilt. These include radio buttons, layout managers, list views, labels, buttons etc.,.
- android.webkit – this library consists of classes which are intended to allow the web browsing capabilities. These will be built into the apps.

These are the core Java-based library is used in the android runtime. Now we will look at the C and C++ Best libraries that are present in this Android software stack layer.

Android Runtime

The runtime of the android consists of the Dalvik Virtual Machine. This virtual machine is used for embedded devices and like any other virtual machine, this is also a bytecode interpreter. The virtual machines for the embedded systems have low memory. They are also slow and are run on battery. The Java libraries, which are core libraries, are also included in this and all the devices can use them.

Kernel

The Linux Kernel 2.6 is used for deriving the android operating system. It is compiled for the electronic equipment. The process Management and memory management are similar to the Linux operating system's process management and a memory management. Between the android software stack and the hardware, the kernel behaves like a hardware abstraction layer. The essential hardware drivers like display, keypad, camera etc., are included in this and it provides abstraction between the hardware to an extent. The kernel also handles things like a vast array of device drivers and networking. The Linux operating system is good at such things. This will help in interfacing to the hardware (peripheral).

To an android app, the essential building blocks are the application components and these are a loosely coupled to AndroidManifest.xml, which is the application manifest file. This file describes every component of the application and it also tells you how they interact.

Within an android app, four components can be used and they are.

Components	Description
Activities	This handles the user interactions with the smartphone display and they dictate the UI.
Services	All the background process and that is associated with an android application are handled by the services.
Broadcast	The broadcast receivers handle the

Receivers	communication between the applications and the android operating system.
Content Providers	Content providers are the ones who handle the database management issues and the data.

Activities

An activity is used for representing a single screen, with a user interface. The actions on the screen are performed by Activity, in short. For instance, an email app might have an activity that displays the list of all the new emails, a different activity is used for composing a new email and another for viewing the email. An application normally consists of multiple activities and in such cases one activity will be used for representing the application when it is launched.

The class Activity can be used for implementing an activity. All the other activities are considered as the subclasses of the Activity class. You can implement an activity as follows:

```
public class MainActivity extends Activity {

}
```

Services

Long running operations are performed by a component called Service that runs in the background. For instance, a service might be playing music from your device in the background while the user is using another application. A service might be fetching data from a network without interrupting the user interaction with an activity.

The class Service can be used for implementing a service. All the other services are considered as the subclasses of the Service class. You can implement a service as follows:

```
public class MyService extends Service {

}
```

Broadcast Receivers

The broadcast receivers respond to the broadcast messages sent from a system or from other applications. For instance, some applications send a broadcast messages to other applications and lets them know that data is downloaded and can be used. The broadcast receiver will intercept this message and they can initiate appropriate action.

The class BroadcastReceiver can be used for implementing a broadcast receiver. All the other broadcast receivers are considered as the subclasses of the BroadcastReceiver class. Every message will be broadcasted as an Intent object. You can implement a broadcast receivers follows:

```
public class MyReceiver  extends  BroadcastReceiver {

  public void onReceive(context,intent){}

}
```

Content Providers

On request, the content provider component will supply the data from an application to others. The ContentResolver class uses its methods for handling such requests. The supplied data may be stored in a database, in the file system or someplace else entirely.

All the content providers are considered as the subclasses of the ContentProvider class. For implementing a content provider you must implement standard set of APIs which, enables other apps to perform transactions.

```
public class MyContentProvider extends  ContentProvider {

  public void onCreate
(){}

}
```

Additional Components

There are a few additional components with which you can construct the mentioned entities above, the wiring between them and their logic. These components are.

Components	Description
Fragments	In an activity, a portion of the user interface is represented by fragments.

Views   All the on-screen drawn UI elements, including
               lists forms, buttons etc.

Layouts   These are the view hierarchies that control the
               appearance and screen format of the views.

Intents   These are the messages that wire the components
               together.

Resources   Resources are the external elements like drawable
               pictures, strings and constants.

Manifest   Manifest is the application's configuration file.

Chapter 3: Android Software Development

The android software development is nothing but a process with which you can create new applications for the android operating system. Usually, Java is used for developing the applications with the android SDK. Don't worry if you are not a Java user. There are many other development environments available. The android SDK consists of a comprehensive set of tools for developing. These include libraries, debugger, QEMU based handset emulator, tutorials, sample code and documentation. The development platforms that are supported currently include systems running on the Linux (any desktop distribution), Windows XP or a later and Mac OS X 10.5.8 or later. For editing the XML and Java files, developers can make use of any text editor and later use the command line tools for creating, building and debugging the android apps. The developers can also control the attached android devices. For using the command line tools, the Apache Ant and the Java Development Kit are required.

With the android platform development, the enhancements to the android software development kit go hand-in-hand. In cases where the developers wish to develop Applications for previous versions of android, they can use the previous versions of the android platform. They are supported by the SDK as well. The development tools can be downloaded and for compatibility testing, previous versions of the platforms and tools can be downloaded after the latest versions.

The android apps will be packed in .apk format. And they will be stored under the folder /data/app on the android operating system. For security purposes, this folder can only be accessed by the root user. The APK package consists of the resource files, .dex files, etc,. The .dex files are compiled in bytecode and are called the Dalvik executables.

Android SDK

We all know that android operating system is an open source. It means that the source code of the android operating system is available to all and it is called as the Android SDK. Anyone can download it, work on android and build a number of different ways. There is no need to download all of it if you only wish to develop an android application. You can use the Android Developer Tools ADT plug-in in the Eclipse IDE. You can select a specific SDK and install it. You can launch emulators, create projects and can debug.

Memory Requirements

Before starting a project, it is wise to look at the memory requirements. The android SDK is 8.5GB in size and for building it, you will need a free space of 30GB.

Prerequisite Installations

Before downloading the software development kit and are starting the cross compiling there are a few prerequisites that you need to have. You should send them first before using the software development kit software. Compared to debugging, prevention is a much better option. Android software development is the android version that we will be using.

Android software development

The android software development is nothing but a process with which you can create new applications for the android operating system. Usually, Java is used for developing the applications with the android SDK. Don't worry if you are not a Java user. There are many other development environments available. The android SDK consists of a comprehensive set of tools for developing. These include libraries, debugger, QEMU based handset emulator, tutorials, sample code and documentation. The development platforms that are supported currently include systems running on the Linux (any desktop distribution), Windows XP or a later and Mac OS X 10.5.8 or later. For editing the XML and Java files, developers can make use of any text editor and later use the command line tools for creating, building and debugging the android apps. The developers can also control the attached android devices. For using the command line tools, the Apache Ant and the Java Development Kit are required.

With the android platform development, the enhancements to the android software development kit go hand-in-hand. In cases where the developers wish to develop Applications for previous versions of android, they can use the previous versions of the android platform. They are supported by the SDK as well. The development tools can be downloaded and for compatibility testing, previous versions of the platforms and tools can be downloaded after the latest versions.

The android apps will be packed in .apk format. And they will be stored under the folder /data/app on the android operating system. For security purposes, the root user can only access this folder. The APK package consists of the resource files, .dex files, etc,. The .dex files are compiled in bytecode and are called the Dalvik executables.

Android Debug Bridge

The Android Debug Bridge or the ADB, in short is nothing but a toolkit, which is included in the software development kit package for android. This toolkit contains both the client side and server side programs which can communicate with each other. The Android Debug Bridge can be accessed using the command line interface and a number of GUIs. Most of the developers only use the command line interface for accessing the Android Debug Bridge. For issuing commands, the following format is used:

adb [-d|-e|-s <serialNumber>] <command>

Fastboot

Diagnostic protocols are used for modifying the flash file system. Fastboot is such diagnostic protocol. It is included in the software development kit package and it is primarily used for modifying the flash filesystem. This is done through a USB connection from the host system. For this, the device must be started on a Secondary Program Loader mode or in a boot loader. Here, only the basic hardware initialization can be performed. Once the protocol is enabled on the device, it will accept a specific set of commands which can be sent through a USB. These commands will be sent using a command line. Here are some of the fastboot commands, which are frequently used.

- flash: Flash will rewrite a partition using the binary image which is stored on the host system.
- erase: Using erase, specific partitions can be erased.
- reboot: The reboot command is used for rebooting the device into its boot loader or into the main OS (the recovery partition of the system).
- format: This command is used for formatting a specific partition. For formatting, the partition's file system must be a recognized one.
- devices: The device command will display the list of all the devices that are connected to the host system along with their serial numbers.

Android Native Development Kit (NDK)

Libraries can be written in programming languages like C, C++ and others, these libraries can be compiled to Microprocessor without Interlocked Pipeline Stages (MIPS), Acorn RISC Machine (ARM) or the x86 native code. These compiled library is can be installed by using the NDK. From the Java code, the native classes can be called under the Dalvik VM, by making use of the System.loadLibrary call. The System.loadLibrary call is a part of the standard Android Java classes.

Are using the traditional development tools, you can compile and install the applications. According to the documentation, the native development kit should not be solely used for application development as the developer only uses C or C++. This will only increase the complexity and most of the apps would not benefit using it.

The android debug Bridge allows you to use a root shell with the android emulator. With this, you can upload and execute of the native code of x86, MIPS and ARM. You can compile the native code using the Intel C++ compiler or GCC if you are using a common PC. However, running this native code without using non-standard to C libraries is complicated. Skia Graphics Library (SGL), is the graphic library used to control access and arbitrate the device. This is also released under the open source license. The UNIX and Win32 support Skia. With this, cross-platform application development is possible. This is also the graphics engine used with the Google's Google chrome Web browser.

The native development Kate is completely based on the command line tools. This is different from the Java application development, which is based on IDE's like eclipse. The command line of the native development kit should be manually in deploying, building and debugging the applications. There are a number of third-party tools that allow the integration of the native development kit with Visual studio and Eclipse.

Android Open Accessory Development Kit

The android platform 3.1, which is also back ported to the platform 2.3.4, introduced the android open accessory support. With this, external hardware like USB can interact with the devices powered by android. For this, the device should be used in the accessory mode. When a device running on android is used in the accessory mode, the accessory connected to it acts like the USB device. The USB exercise of android designed specifically to attach the devices running on android with a simple protocol that allows the detection of android devices supporting the accessory mode.

Native Go support

From the 1.4 version of the programming language Go, Application development for android without requiring Java code is supported. However, you are restricted to use a set of APIs.

Third-party development tools

App Inventor for Android

The app inventor for android is a visual development environment based on the web. This is for novice programmers. The app inventor for android is based on the Open Blocks Java Library of MIT. This can provide access to the phone functions, GPS, orientation and accelerometer data, speech to text conversion, web services, text messaging, persistent storage, contact data etc,. Twitter and Amazon were initially included too. Google released the source code in the second half of 2011 and they terminated its a web service.

Basic4android

Basic4android is a product commercially available in the market. This is similar to the simple and is inspired by the visual studio and a Visual Basic 6 of Microsoft. Android programming is made simpler for Microsoft Visual Basic programmers who find it difficult to code in Java. Basic4android has a very strong online community because of its activeness. Many developers offer online help in the community.

Corona SDK

The corona the founder of Corona labs Inc creates SDK... He is Mr. Walter Luh. Using the Corona Software Development Kit, programmers can develop applications for android and iOS devices like iPad and iPhone.

By making use of the corona SDK Lua language, developers can create graphical applications. The Lua language is integrated with the SDK. It's a language is on top of the openGL/C++ layers. A subscription based purchased model is used by the SDK. No branding charges or per app royalty are required.

Delphi

You can use Delphi for creating object Pascal android applications. Embarcadero developed the latest Delphi version XE8.

HyperNext Android Creator

If you are a software developer who is not very good at Java or if you cannot use the Android SDK, you can create your own android applications using the software development system called the HyperNext Android Creator. This development system is mainly aimed for programming beginners. We all know that the applications on mobile only display one window at a time. This software development system is based on that principle. It makes use of the HyperCard. HyperCard treats given software as a stack of cards. At a given point of time, only a single card can be visible. This makes it suitable for mobile applications. The main programming language of the HyperNext Android Creator is called HyperNext. HyperNext is based loosely on the HyperTalk language of HyperCard. It is English like interpreted language. It offers many features which allow the developers in creating android applications. The HyperNext android creator supports a wide range of android SDK which includes their own version of the graphical user interface control types. This will run as a background service of its own in the background so that the applications can process information and continue running in the background.

Kivy

Kivy is natural user interface application software used for developing touch applications. This is a python library and is open source. Using Kivy, it is possible to maintain a single application for multiple operating systems. This follows the code once and run everywhere concept. Kivy includes Buildozer, which is the development tool custom built for deploying mobile apps. Buildozer is only available for the Linux operating system. It is an alpha software and compare that to the older deployment methods of Kivy, it is far less cumbersome. The applications that are programmed using Kivy can be used on any mobile App distribution platform for android.

Lazarus

You can develop applications using the object Pascal with the Lazarus IDE. This is based on the Pascal compiler from the version 2.7.1. This is available free of cost.

Processing

This is a processing environment that uses Java. It started its support from the android version 1.5. You can use the Ketai library for integrating with the sensors and device camera.

Qt for Android

The Qt is a framework that can work on multiple platforms and it can target platforms like LINUX, windows, Sailfish OS and android. The application development of Qt is done in the standard QML and C++. Qt requires both the android SDK and NDK.

RubyMotion

For writing need to mobile applications in Ruby, the RubyMotion tool chain can be used. From the 3.0 version of RubyMotion, Android is supported. The entire set of the Java android APIs can be called by the RubyMotion Android applications from Ruby. Third-party Java libraries can be used and these are compiled into machine code statistically.

SDL

Besides Java, the SDL library also offers the development possibilities for C programming and simple porting for native C applications and existing SDL. By injecting JNI and small Java shim, it is possible to use the native SDL code. This allows ports like the video game Jagged Alliance 2.

Visual Studio 2015

The cross platform development is supported by the 2015 Visual studio. With this, C++ developers can create the projects using templates for the android native activity applications. High-performance shared libraries can also be created and these can be included in other solutions. Devices deployment, platform-specific IntelliSense, emulation and breakpoints are some of its features.

Xamarin

Using a C# shared CodeBase, the developers can use the Xamarin for writing the native android applications with native UI. Xamarin also shares the code across different platforms.

Java standards

Android OS doesn't use the Java SE and ME, which are established Java standards. This fact is an obstacle to development. The compatibility of the Java applications designed for other platforms is not possible. Android reuses the syntax and semantics of the tower language. Though it uses them, it doesn't support the APIs and full class libraries with the Java ME or SE. You can add Java MA to the conversion services of android using some tools. These tools are released into the market by companies like UpOnTek and Myriad group.

Rooting

Rooting can be defined as the process which provides the uses of tablets, smartphones and other devices which runs on the android mobile OS, which gives the users privileged control for different android systems. This control is called root access. As the android operating system is based on the Linux kernel, similar administrator permissions will be given after rooting an android device.

If you wish to overcome the limitations set by the carriers or hardware manufacturers, android rooting is the thing to do. You can replace or alter the settings and applications by rooting. You will have permissions at admin level with which you can perform operations that cannot be performed by normal users. With the recent release, you can completely replace or remove the operating system on the device using rooting.

Many people think that rooting is equivalent to jail breaking the Apple iOS. This is not true and they are two completely different concepts. Jail breaking gives the users access to prohibited areas which may include modification of the OS, installing applications by side loading, which are not officially approved etc,. On the other hand, android routing grants the user with elevated admin level privileges. Only a few of the android devices prohibit users from accessing the boot loaders. Most of the vendors like Sony, Google, Asus and HTC provide the ability to unlock the device explicitly. The users can even change the operating system of the device entirely.

Routing allows all the applications installed by the user to run the privileged commands. These privileged commands are not available for stock configuration devices. Rooting requires potentially dangerous and advanced operations like deleting or modifying the system files, uninstalling manufacturer or carrier installed applications and accessing the hardware (calibrating touch input, controlling status lights or rebooting). Any typical rooting installation installs super user application. This super user application supervises all the other applications which are granted with the super user or root rights. Request for approval will be granted for user for permissions. The device's boatload patient will also be unlocked and it is required to replace all remove the operating system installed.

Compared to the jail breaking of iOS, Android routing is not necessary for running the applications published by developers outside the play store. This is sometimes called side loading. This feature is supported by the android operating system into ways. They are by the Android Debug Bridge and by the unknown sources option present in the settings.

Android routing allows the users to delete or modify the system files. This allows The users to use applications which require root access and to perform various tweaks.

Advantages

Complete control over the feel and look of the device one of the advantages included in android rooting. The user will become a super user and he is allowed to access the system files on the device and he can also customize the aspects of the OS. The only limitation is the coding expertise. The following are the expected advantages of android rooting.

Super users are given full theming capabilities. It means that they can change everything from the look of Dialer, the look of the contact list, colors and themes, notification lights, battery indicator color and even the format of videos that he can play on the device while the device boots.

The user gets full control of the kernel and CPU.

Full control to the applications will be given which include the capability to restore, backup, remove pre-installed bloat ware, edit batch applications etc,.

Applications like Tasker can be used for automating the processes on the device.

Android rooting permits the users to install their own custom firmware. Custom firmware provides additional control on the device. Since the android operating system is open source, any programmer with good skills can customize their version of android.

Android Dev Phone

The Android Dev Phone, ADP, is nothing but a boot loader unlocked and SIM unlocked device running on android designed for advanced developers. Developers can purchase the regular android devices available in the market and can use them to test the applications that they have developed. Most of the developers do not go with devices on the market as they are locked. Most of the developers prefer using an unlocked device. The Nexus series of Google is now providing the development phones. The Nexus devices available come with good hardware configurations.

Applications that are distributed on the Google play store can be copyrighted by the publisher. This will prevent users from using the application's source code. This action will be disabled in the case of the Android Dev Phones as they come with unrestricted access to the operating system. Applications with copyright protection will not be displayed on the Google play store for the Android Dev Phones.

You can start developing your android application on any of the following OSs.

- Microsoft Windows XP or later version.
- Mac OS X 10.5.8 or later version with Intel chip.
- Linux including GNU C Library 2.7 or later.

For developing android applications, you will be requiring all the tools and these tools are available free of cost and you can download them from the web. The list of software that are required for android application programming are given below.

- Android Development Tools (ADT) Eclipse Plug-in (optional)
- Java Runtime Environment (JRE) 6
- Java JDK5 or later version
- Android SDK
- Android Studio
- Eclipse IDE for Java Developers (optional)

The Eclipse plug-in and the eclipse IDE are optional. Using them on the system running Windows operating system will be helpful with the application development based on Java.

Chapter 4 – How to Become an Android App Developer from Scratch

You can't just sit down one day and decide that you are going to develop and app for Android. There are certain things you must do to prepare yourself, so here goes:

1. Learn How a Computer Works

This is one of these unavoidable steps because, let's face it, if you are going to be developing apps, you need to have some idea of how a computer works. Now, you don't need to know everything but you do need to know how the computer actually works, how a program works, what that program is made of and you need to understand some of the basic terminology used in the industry – bits, bytes, conditionals, loops, etc. So, your first step is to do a little research and familiarize yourself with these things.

2. Learn Object Oriented Programming and Java

In the first step, you should have learned some of the basics so now it's time to dig that little bit deeper and find out how today's programs have been written with speed and efficiency in mind. You must learn Java programming because that is the core of the Android language.

Java is widely used so you won't find it difficult to get a handle on it and, once you have learnt some it, move on to object oriented programming. When you understand how both of these work, you are ready to start narrowing it down to the world of Android.

3. The Android SDK and the Developers Website

You now know a bit about how computers and programs work and you have learnt something about Java and object oriented programming. You are now ready to get into the finer points of developing an app for Android. One of the best things about Android development is that just about everything you need is packaged up neatly into one SDK or Software Development Kit. Like other platforms, Android also comes with an optimized IDE – Integrated Development Environment so all you need to do is familiarize yourself with the methods and the tools that Android supplies you.

The most important thing, something that is very effective, is learning what you can about Android's architecture. Each platform is different in the way it does things so you should get yourself up to scratch with the basics – it will help your efficiency and code writing in the future as well.

4. Practice Makes Perfect

Nothing will improve your skills as much as doing as many projects as you possibly can. Any time you want to learn something, set up a project and start looking at it in parts. That way you will learn more and you can apply to the project directly from the learning materials that are supplied for you. Not only will this give you a learning edge, it will also save you time.

Chapter 5 - Getting Started

So, how do you go about developing for Android? First, let's look at the overview:

- You will write your program, whatever you want your app to do. These are written in Java and then your layout is designed, depending on how you want that app to look, in XML files.
- When your app is ready, you will be able to use a supplied build tool to put all the files together into one .apk file. This is what will run on your Android device and is what you send to Google Play for acceptance into the store.
- Every file that you produced is manage through the IDE and this is also where you can edit code files as well as managing all of your projects.
- Eclipse used to be the IDE for Android but this is gradually being phased out and replaced by Android Studio, owned by Google

That's a basic overview so let's get a deeper look behind the scenes. The idea of this next part of the book I to have you download the necessary software and set up a very simple app to test it all out, as well as making a couple of edits to that app. This will give you a bit of hands on experience so that, when we get to actually building an app you will know what it's all about. And yes, by the end of this book, you will have built an app that records any message that you care to type, puts it in a list and saves it, before sharing it. You will also learn how to configure parts of the user interface. Before all that, we need to get the software downloaded.

Installing Android Studio

While you might, be getting excited and want to jump straight in and write some code, you really need to get your environment set up first. Take your time with this section and make sure you follow each step exactly. Even doing this, you might still have a few small issues that you will have to troubleshoot, depending on the product versions you are using or your system configuration.

At this stage, it is very important that you do not let anything stop you from progressing in your quest to learn Android so take any setbacks in your stride and learn from them before you move on to the next stage.

So, the next step is to look and see if you have the JDK – Java Development Kit – installed. It might already be on your computer; you just don't know it! To check this out, you need to use Terminal – this is how you get to know your computer, how you command it to do what you want and it's very easy to use. How do you find it on your computer?

- On a Mac, use Spotlight to search for Terminal and choose the top search result.
- On a PC, click on Start, Run, type in cmd and press enter

It's as easy as that.

Once the terminal is open, at the command prompt, type **java-version**. You will see one of two things – either an output that tells you which version of Java you are running or a message that says **command not found** – this means that JDK is not installed on your computer. If it isn't, head to Oracle and download the JDK.

When you have done that, head to Android Studio and download the right version for the operating system you are running.

When Android Studio has downloaded successfully, open it up. You will get a Setup Wizard popup appear the first time so click on **Next** to get to the next screen. You now need to choose the setup type that you want, click on **standard** and then click **Next.** Click to accept the license agreements and click **Next** for the final time. Android Studio will now download all the extra bits and pieces that you need. This should take no more than a few minutes.

Make sure that you are running the latest version of Android Studio by clicking on **Check for Updates** at the bottom of the screen. If any later versions appear, click on **Update and Restart**.

That's it! Android Studio is installed and ready for use.

Chapter 6 - The Android SDK Manager

Each Android version contains its own SDK for you to use when building your app. The setup wizard will make sure that you are able to access the most up to date version. Now, one of the things the SDK lets you do is to set up an AVD – Android Virtual Device. This is what you can test your newly built app on and you can customize it to your personal configuration. We'll talk more about those later on but, first, let's get to grips with Android Studio.

On the Welcome screen, click on **Configure.** You will now see a new menu with lots of different options. The one you want is called **SDK Manager** so click on it and a new window will appear, with a series of folders and checkboxes, as well as statuses.

You should already be running the latest version of the SDK Tools, Platform-Tools and the Build-Tools. Look at the checkbox beside each of these tools; f an update is available, the box will be ticked, and there will be a message in Status telling you that there is another version and what it is.

For the purposes of this tutorial, I want you to download the previous Android version, Android 4.4.2. Click on the box next to the icon for 4.4.2, thus selecting the entire contents of the directory for download. Later on, you can come back to SDK Manager to delete anything that you don't need.

Click on **Install x Packages (**x denoted the number of packages that are selected for download**).** You will find this on the bottom right hand side of the SDK Manager. Another window will show up and that will have a drop down menu, showing a list of all the packages you are installing. All you do here is click on the root of the drop down menu and click on **Accept License** – the button is down in the bottom right of the screen. Depending on the packages you are downloading, you might need to do this a number of times. Lastly, click on **Install**, bottom of the window, to get your downloads going.

The window will shut down and your items will begin to download and install. Leave it to complete, without touching anything. Get used to doing this – it will be a regular thing so that you can stay updated with all the right package versions.

As soon as the SDK Manager has finished its work, you are ready to start creating your very first app for Android.

Chapter 7 - Let's Create OMG Android

It's time to get started on your first project. We're going to start simple, much like the "Hello, World!" program you often see beginners creating. We will follow the tradition of that program and make a few edits along the way so that the app will greet you personally, by name. By the time we have finished you will be able to load the app onto your Android device and show it off to your friends!

Android Studio includes a very nice step-by-step tool that will help you get this project underway so, to start, form the Welcome screen in Studio, click on Start a New Android Studio Project. You will be presented with a project creation screen.

In the field for **Application Name,** type in **OMG Android.** You can put your own name into the **Company Domain** field. As you type, notice that **Package Name** changes to make a reverse domain name, based on your **Company Domain** and **Application Name.**

This name is used as a unique identifier, so that your app can be found in amongst all the others. This way, the work that is done on the app, on a particular Android device, knows its particular source and there is no confusion between two apps that may be named similarly or the same.

Set **Project Location** to your chosen hard drive location and then click on **Next** to go on to the next but of the project.

This next screen is where you start to select the operating systems and devices that you want to target your app to. You don't have to build an app that works on all Android devices; you could narrow it down and make it just for tablets and/or smartphones if you wanted to. For this tutorial, you are going to target an Android phone and you will see that this option is already selected by default, alongside **Minimum SDK**.

The menu for **Minimum SDK** sets the minimum Android version that is needed for your app to run. When you do your own projects, selecting the value is a balancing act between the devices you want your app to support and the SDK capabilities that you want. This time, we will stick with using the default selection, API 16 – Android 4.1 Jelly Bean.

Click on **Next** and another screen will appear, to let you choose an activity for your app. Think of the activity as being a window in your app that shows content that the user interacts with. The activity can be a popup or it can be an entire window.

On this template, the range of activities goes from a blank one that has an **Action Bar** to one that includes an embedded **Map View.** There will be a lot of these so it's good to get used to them.

For this project, select **Blank Activity** and then click **Next.**

You are now on the last screen before you start to get into the actual coding. To hasten things a long a little, we will use the pre-populated default values but first, let's look at what is done with the values:

- **Activity Name** – this gives your activity a name that can be referred to in the code. Once you have finished with the project setup, Studio is going to create a .java class and the contents of the Activity Name is what will give that class its name.
- **Layout Name** – Your activity is going to be defined in Java but the layout is defined in an Android XML. We will be talking about those later on.

Click on **Finish** and Studio will go off and do some stuff behind the scenes to create your first project. Every now and again, it will throw out some descriptions and you might notice your project name and also a word that says **Gradle** and **Maven.** One of the biggest benefits to using Studio, or other modern IDE's is that much is done for you. However, it is still a good idea to learn exactly what these things mean so you know what Android Studio is doing:

- **Gradle** - this is a new build-tool that is dead easy to use. It has a lot of advanced options for those who want to dig deeper. Gradle takes your Java code and your XML layouts and creates an APK file using the latest build tools. You can customize the configurations to created different versions of your app that work differently and you can also add in dependencies for third party libraries.

- **Maven** – this is another build-tool that is also easy to use. In conjunction with Gradle, you can add all kinds of functionality in from the Android Development Community.

Given a couple of minutes, Studio will finish the build of your project. At this stage, your project is pretty much empty but contains all that it needs to be launched on an emulator or Android device.

There are now three windows in Android Studio. On the left is your project folder structure, in the middle is a preview on a Nexus 5 of what your layout looks like and the last window shows the layout hierarchy and the attributes if part of your hierarchy is selected. Before you start any real programming though, we want to get this app running. Let's go and say "Hello, World!"

Chapter 8 - Important Application Files

The below topic will give you an overview on some of the important application files.

The Main Activity File

The main activity cold is nothing but MainActivity.java, a java file. This application file will modify your application by converting into Dalvik executable. Given below is the default code that is generated by the application wizard for the application Hello World!

package com.example.helloworld;

import android.os.Bundle;
import android.app.Activity;
import android.view.Menu;
import android.view.MenuItem;
import android.support.v4.app.NavUtils;

```
public class MainActivity extends Activity {
  @Override
  public void onCreate(Bundle savedInstanceState) {
    super
.onCreate(savedInstanceState);
    setContentView(R.layout.activity_main);
  }

  @
Override
  public boolean onCreateOptionsMenu(Menu menu) {
    getMenuInflater
().inflate(R.menu.activity_main, menu);
    return true;
  }
}
```

In this application, R.layout.activity_main is used for referring the activity_main.xml file present in the res/layoutfolder.

The method onCreate() is one of the many available methods fired during the loading of the application.

The Manifest File

Any component that is the developer develops as a part of the application, must be declared in the manifest.xml. This is it located in the Application project directory root. This will act as an interface between your application and the android operating system. If your components are not declared in this file, they won't be considered by the operating system. Here is an example showing a default manifest file.

```xml
<manifest
xmlns:android="http://schemas.android.com/apk/res/andr
oid"
  package="com.example.helloworld"
  android:versionCode="1"
  android:versionName="1.0" >

  <uses-sdk
    android:minSdkVersion="8"
    android:targetSdkVersion="22" />

  <application
    android:icon="@drawable/ic_launcher"
    android:label="@
string/app_name
"
    android:theme="@style/AppTheme" >
    <activity
      android:name=".MainActivity"
      android:label="@
string/title_activity_main
" >

      <intent-filter>
        <action android:name="android.intent.action.MAIN"
/>
        <category
android:name="android.intent.category.LAUNCHER"/>
      </intent-filter>

    </activity>

  </application>
</manifest>
```

In this example, <application>...</application> tags are used for enclosing the application related components. The android:icon find the available application icon present in the res/drawable-hdpi. An image named ic_launcher.png will be used by the application. This image will be present in the drawable folders.

The tag <activity> is used for specifying an activity. The attribute android:name is it used for specifying a fully qualified class, which is a subclass of the activity subclass. You can use the <activity> tags for specifying the multiple activities.

The action for the intent filter is named android.intent.action.MAIN to indicate that this activity serves as the entry point for the application.The category for the intent-filter is named android.intent.category.LAUNCHER to indicate that the application can be launched from the device's launcher icon.

The @string refers to the strings.xml file explained below.Hence, @string/app_namerefersto the app_name string defined in the strings.xml file, which is"HelloWorld".Similar way, other strings get populated in the application.

You will use the following set of tags for specifying various components of the Android application in your manifest file.

- <activity>elements for activities
- <service> elements for services
- <receiver>elements for broadcast receivers
- <provider>elements for content providers

The Strings File

The file strings.xml is present in the folder res/values. All the text that your app uses will be contained in that file. For instance, default text, labels, buttons and similar strings will be contained in this file. The strings.xml file is responsible for the textual content of your application. The default string file is shown in the given example.

```
<resources>
  <string name="app_name">HelloWorld</string>
  <string name="hello_world">Hello world!</string>
  <string name="menu_settings">Settings</string>
  <string
name="title_activity_main">MainActivity</string>
</resources>
```

The Layout File

The layout file, activity_main.xml is available in the directory res/layout. Whenever your app is building its interface, this file will be referred. For changing the layout of your app, you will need to modify this file frequently. For the application hello world!, The following content will be in the layout file by default, it is given in the examples shown below.

```
<RelativeLayout
xmlns:android="http://schemas.android.com/apk/res/andr
oid"
  xmlns:tools="http://schemas.android.com/tools"
  android:layout_width="match_parent"
  android:layout_height="match_parent"                    >
```

```
<TextView
  android:layout_width="wrap_content"
  android:layout_height="wrap_content"
  android:layout_centerHorizontal="true"
  android:layout_centerVertical="true"
  android:padding="@dimen/padding_medium"
  android:text="@string/hello_world"
  tools:context=".MainActivity"                    />

</RelativeLayout>
```

This is a simple relativelayout example and we will look at it in later chapters.

An android control called TextView is used for building the graphical user interface. It has many attributes like android:layout_height, android:layout_width, etc, attributes are used for setting the height and width etc. The @string is used for referring the strings.XML file. It is located in the folder res/values. The hello string is referred by the @string/hello_world, which is defined in the file strings.xml file. That is in turn the "Hello World!".

Chapter 9 - Running Your App on an Emulator or Device

OK, you have Android studio and you have created your first app. How are you going to run it? If you have an Android device at your disposal, you can use that but you can also use an emulator.

Android Studio includes the ability to set up a software-based device on your computer. This allows you to run apps, look through websites, and debug your app and all sorts of other things. It's called the Android Emulator.

You can set up more than one emulator on your computer and you can set each one to a specific screen size and platform version. This is a good thing because the Android platform is so diverse that, without this ability, you would need to have hundreds of different devices in front of you for testing purposes.

If you followed the instructions for running through the setup wizard earlier, you will already have an emulator ready to use. However, so that you know how to, we are going to set up a new emulator.

Click on **AVD Manager** – look in the toolbar for an icon that shows the Android popping up its head, beside a device that has a purple display. Android Studio already has one of these set up for you to use, you can see some details about it – the type of emulator, the CPU instruction set it uses, and the API it uses.

To create a new AVD, click on **Create Virtual Device**. Now you need to make some choices, the first one being what device type you want it to emulate. On the left is a **category** list that shows all the different types of device that can be emulated. If you click on each option in turn, you can see what devices are available in each category. For this, we want to select a phone-sized device so click on **Phone** category and the choose **Nexus S**. Click on **Next**.

Next, you have to decide on the Android version you want to use. There will already be a couple available so click on **Lollipop** and check that the **ABI** column shows the value **x86.** This is to ensure that the emulator runs as fast as it can on an x86 computer. Click on **Next** to go on to the last screen.

This is simply a confirmation screen, showing your choices and giving you the option to configure other device properties, such as the device name, RAM size and startup orientation. For now, just stick to the default selections and click on **Finish.**

You have now created a new virtual device to test out your app on.

Shut down AVD Manager and go back to the main screen on Android Studio. There is just one final step – click on **Run**. The button looks like a typical "play" icon.

Another window will show up and you will be asked to pick the device that you want to test the app on. At this stage, you don't have any devices running so you can start the AVD you created earlier. Make sure the button for **Launch Emulator** is checked and that your AVD has been selected from the drop down menu; click on **OK.**

Wait a while to give the emulator time to load and be prepared to have to do this a few times until the emulator gets it right. Once it's finished you will be able to see what there is of your app running.

Let's Put the Personal Touch to Your App

So, you have your first app but, let's be honest here, what I the one thing you would like to do, something you would want to do with any of your work? Put your name to it!

Go to res/values/strings.xml and then double click on the file. Now we are going to change the hello_world string – this is the one that is actually displayed on your screen so we need to change it to something personal, something that has your name in it. Something along the lines of:

- <string name="hello_world">Darryl is learning Android!</string>

Obviously, you would insert your own name here.

Click on Run and when your app has launched, you will see your own message on the screen.

Congratulations! You have successfully built an app, and edited it to show off a personalized message.

Chapter 10: Organize Resources In Android Studio

There are several other items that you can make use for building an android application. You can manage other resources apart from your application code, like the resources. These resources include animation instructions, user interface strings, layout definitions, colors, bitmaps, etc,. All of these resources will be maintained in separate subdirectories. They will be placed in the directory res/ of your project.

```
MyProject/
  src/
    main/
    java/
      MyActivity.java
  res/
    drawable/
      icon.png
    layout/
      activity_main.xml
      info.xml
```

```
values/
  strings.xml
```

Alternative Resources

Alternative resources should be provided by your application for supporting specific device configurations. For instance, alternate drawable resources should be included for supporting different resolutions of different screens, you should provide different string resources as alternatives for different languages. Android will detect the current system configuration during runtime and will load the required resources for the application to run.

Here is an example where the images are given specifically for default screen resolution. Alternate images are also given for screens with higher resolutions.

```
MyProject/
 src/
    main/
    java/
      MyActivity.java
    res/
      drawable/
       icon.png
       background.png
     drawable-hdpi/
       icon.png
       background.png
     layout/
       activity_main.xml
       info.xml
     values/
       strings.xml
```

In the below example, a specific layout is given for the default language and for Arabic, an alternate layout is given.

```
MyProject/
 src/
    main/
    java/
      MyActivity.java
   res/
     drawable/
       icon.png
       background.png
     drawable-hdpi/
       icon.png
       background.png
     layout/
       activity_main.xml
       info.xml
     layout-ar/
       main.xml
     values/
       strings.xml
```

Accessing Resources

You'll need to access different defined resources during the development of your application in your XML file layout or in the app's code. This section will explain you how your resources can be accessed in the two scenarios.

Accessing Resources in Code

After the compilation of your Android application, a class R will be generated and it will have the resource IDs for all of the available resources present in your res/ directory. You can make use of the R class for accessing those resources by providing the resource ID or by giving the subdirectory and resource name. Here is an example.

Example

For accessing res/drawable/myimage.png and for setting an ImageView you will use the code given below.

```
ImageView imageView = (ImageView)
findViewById(R.id.myimageview);
imageView.setImageResource(R.drawable.myimage);
```

The first line of the above code will use the R.id.myimageview for getting the ImageView that is defined with id myimageview from the layout file. In the second line, the R.drawable.myimage is used for getting the myimage image. This will make the image available under the /res drawable subdirectory. Here is an example.

Example

Consider the following examples where res/values/strings.xml has the given definition.

```
<?xml version="1.0" encoding="utf-8"?>
<resources>
  <string name="hello">Hello, World!</string>
</resources>
```

Using the ID msg or resource ID, text can be set on the TextView object. The code is given.

TextView msgTextView = (TextView)
findViewById(R.id.msg);
msgTextView.setText(R.string.hello);

Example

Consider the layout res/layout/activity_main.xml with the given definition.

```xml
<?xml version="1.0" encoding="utf-8"?>
<LinearLayout
xmlns:android="http://schemas.android.com/apk/res/android"
  android:layout_width="fill_parent"
  android:layout_height="fill_parent"
  android:orientation="vertical" >

  <TextView android:id="@+id/text"
    android:layout_width="wrap_content"
    android:layout_height="wrap_content"
    android:text="
Hello, I am a TextView
" />

  <Button android:id="@+id/button"
    android:layout_width="wrap_content"
    android:layout_height="wrap_content"
    android:text="
Hello, I am a Button
" />

</LinearLayout>
```

This layout will be loaded by the application code for an activity. This will be loaded in the method onCreate(), as given below.

```
public void onCreate(Bundle savedInstanceState) {
  super.onCreate(savedInstanceState);
  setContentView(R.layout.main_activity);
}
```

Accessing Resources in XML

For this example, we will consider the given resource file, res/values/strings.xml. A string resource and a colour resource are included in that file.

```
<?xml version="1.0" encoding="utf-8"?>
<resources>
  <color name="opaque_red">#f00</color>
  <string name="hello">Hello!</string>
</resources>
```

You can now use of these resources in the layout file given below and can set the text string and text color as follows.

```
<?xml version="1.0" encoding="utf-8"?>
<EditText
xmlns:android="http://schemas.android.com/apk/res/android"
  android:layout_width="fill_parent"
  android:layout_height="fill_parent"
  android:textColor="@color/opaque_red"
  android:text="@string/hello" />
```

Chapter 11 - Updating With the SDK Manager

This is going to work no matter what SDK version you downloaded but it is good practice to keep your versions up to date. To open the SDK Manager from within your project, click on the button that shows a downward arrow with an Android peeking above it. By the time you have completed this section, you will have an app that has:

- A PNG image
- A text field that is editable so you can write a message
- A button that lets you submit your input
- A text view that will display the last message
- A list displaying all messages
- The option to share your message on Social Networking sites, such as Facebook and Twitter, through email and though SMS.

- A greeting that, whenever you open the app, will retrieve your name

At this point, you should have the "Hello, World!" app open and running on your device or the emulator, showing off your personalized message. Let's take it to the next level.

Getting Started

Let's just look ahead for a minute – the very first thing you have to do is make sure that your app is going to be as simple as it possibly can. There is no need at this stage to introduce any extra complexity unless it is absolutely necessary – it takes more time and more work and that's something you don't need at the moment.

First of all, open up **app/res/layout/activity_main.xml** – can you see the raw .raw .xml fie? If you can all is well; if not you will need to switch to Text mode that you can do at the bottom of the screen.

All we are going to do here is get rid of some of the padding attributes that Studio generates in your .xml file automatically. They will look a little like this:

- android:paddingLeft="@dimen/activity_horizontal_margin"
- android:paddingRight="@dimen/activity_horizontal_margin"

- android:paddingTop="@dimen/activity_vertical_mar gin"
- android:paddingBottom="@dimen/activity_vertical_ margin"

Delete all of these lines; your activity.xml file should look like this now:

- <RelativeLayout xmlns:android="http://schemas.android.com/apk/re s/android"
- xmlns:tools="http://schemas.android.com/tools"
- android:layout_width="match_parent"
- android:layout_height="match_parent"
- tools:context=".MainActivity">
-
- <TextView
- android:text="@string/hello_world"
- android:layout_width="wrap_content"
- android:layout_height="wrap_content" />
-
- </RelativeLayout>

Double click on **Mainactivity.java -** you will find it on the left pane in Studio – and let's take a look at your very first piece of code. You will need to remove the following lines:

- @Override
- public   boolean   onOptionsItemSelected(MenuItem

item) {
- // Handle action bar item clicks here. The action bar will
- // automatically handle clicks on the Home/Up button, so long
- // as you specify a parent activity in AndroidManifest.xml.
- int id = item.getItemId();
-
- //noinspection SimplifiableIfStatement
- if (id == R.id.action_settings) {
- return true;
- }
-
- return super.onOptionsItemSelected(item);
- }

Be extra careful that you leave the last curly brace in place – this is the one that closes the class.

Now that you have finished your housekeeping, it really is time to get started and give your **Activity** a life of its own.

Chapter 12 - XML Layout Basics

Android layouts are all in the XML format, which looks like a tree with one root and a hierarchy of views. This hierarchy is straightforward and it is strict – each view is called the Parent of all the views contained in it and the Child of the view that contains it.

Open up **res/layout/activity_main.xml** – this is where you will see your activity XML here. There is a parent called **Relative Layout** and a child called **TextView.**

Have a look at **TextView.** You should be able to see that it has three attributes in t – two of these will be in every view you will ever use in an Android layout and they are **layout_width** and **layout_height.** The values for both of these may take a number of forms:

- **wrap_content** – this is a constant value that specifies the view will be big enough to just fit in what is required to go in it, be it a text, image or child view.
- **match_parent** – this is another constant that will

set the view to be as large as its parent

- **Explicit values** - you can set the dimension to a set number of pixels, i.e. 5px, but it you should really use density independent pixels, for example 5dp. On a medium density device, a dp is a pixel. The actual amount of pixels will scale for those devices that are designated and high density, low density, extra high density, etc.

In other words, if you used straight pixels, your views would be all manner of strange sizes, depending on whether the device it is on is 160 pixels per inch (ppi) or 300, or anything in between. Allow the system to sort out the scaling and use dp.

The third attributes called **text** and this is when the text that will be displayed is specified. This is an excellent example of how a different view will respond to a different attribute. If you added in a **text** attribute to **Space** or a **RelativeLayout**, it would make no difference whatsoever because, they would not know what to do with it, unlike the **TextView**, which would.

However, the attribute value, **@string/hello_world** is not what is on show, Whatever you specify n the layout file does not translate to the string that s displayed, instead it is a string ID that identifies the proper text. This way, you can keep all of your app copy in one single place – in **res/values/strings/xl.**

Next, we are going to look at the **RelativeLayout** parent node in XML.

Relative Layouts

When Android Studio created your default project, it set you up with a very useful layout, called **RelativeLayout.** This is the parent layout and the **TextView** element is the child.

Linear Layouts

LinearLayout should have specified orientations, either vertical or horizontal. Once that has been done, it will line up all of its children in the chosen orientation, in the order the XML specifies.

LinearLayout children do not respond to attributes like **Layout_toRightOf;** instead, they will respond to **layout_weight** and **layout_gravity.** When you specify a **layout_weight** you are expanding the view to a set proportion of the parent. In this way, the weight of the parent is equal to the sum of all the child weights. Confused? Read on and I will try to explain this a bit better.

Look at how the height of the parent view is split between all the child views, based on whatever weight is assigned to a particular child. If you were to assign a **layout_gravity** to a view, you would be setting the vertical and horizontal positions in the parent **LinearLayout.** For example, one view may have a **Layout_gravity** attribute that has a value like **left, right** and **center vertical.** You can also combine previous values, like this - **top|center_horizontal.** And then there is **gravity**, which you should not get confused with **layout_gravity.**

The latter is where you place the view but the attribute **gravity** defines how the content of the view is placed in the view. If you want your text to be set in a particular way, i.e., centered, left or right, you need to use **gravity.**

There is one handy thing you should know and that is that you can nest layouts inside one another. However, you do not want your layouts to be too layered so if yours begin to look as though they are getting out of hand, switch over to a **relative_layout.**

Before you move on, open up **res/layout/activity_main.xml** and we are going to make a change her. The root node must be changed from a **RelativeLayout** – defined by Android Studio as default – to a **LinearLayout.** You need to replace the following lines:

- <RelativeLayout xmlns:android="http://schemas.android.com/apk/res/android"
- xmlns:tools="http://schemas.android.com/tools"
- android:layout_width="match_parent"
- android:layout_height="match_parent"
- tools:context=".MainActivity">

And this one that you will find at the very end of the file:

- </RelativeLayout>

With this:

- <LinearLayout xmlns:android="http://schemas.android.com/apk/res/android"
- xmlns:tools="http://schemas.android.com/tools"
- android:layout_width="match_parent"
- android:layout_height="match_parent"
- android:orientation="vertical"
- tools:context=".MainActivity">
- </LinearLayout>

Accessing Views From Within Java

Ok, so Layouts are most the domain of the XML fil but there are lots of other visual elements that you might want to create, change, even destroy from your Java code.

First, we need to edit the **TextView** that you will find in **activity-main.xml** so that it looks like this:

- <TextView
- android:id="@+id/main_textview"
- android:layout_width="wrap_content"

- android:layout_height="wrap_content"
- android:layout_marginLeft="20dp"
- android:layout_marginTop="20dp"
- android:text="@string/hello_world"/>

Did you notice that we added in a new attribute - **id.** By using this attribute, or tag, you can access the specified **View** from your code and this lets you manipulate that **view** via your code in the future.

We also need to make a change in the **text** tag. The string resource name is **hello_world**, which is a bit outdated to be far. So, right click on **@string/hello_world** (it's only a part of the line so click on the right bit) and then select **Refactor** and **Rename.**

Next, type the world **textview** in and click on **Refactor.**

This is going to do two things – change the resource ID name in the layout file and the original resource ID that is in your **strings.xml** file. It will also change the name of the resource wherever else it shows up throughout your project.

Open up **MainActivity.java** and add in the following line – make sure it goes above **onCreate** method and below the **MainActivity** class declarations:

- TextView mainTextView;

At this point, we have not yet imported the **TextView** class into **MainActivity.java** so it is not aware of what a **TextView** is. That is easily fixed with Android Studio. All you need to do is tap **Alt+Enter** on your computer keyboard while the error message popup is on the screen – this will import **TextView** for you.

The next thing to do is add the following code into onCreate, inserting it after the two lines of code that are already in there:

- // 1. Access the TextView defined in layout XML
- // and then set its text
- mainTextView = (TextView) findViewById(R.id.main_textview);
- mainTextView.setText("Set in Java!");

Take a look at the **MainActivity.java** file – it should look like this:

- public class MainActivity extends ActionBarActivity {
-
- TextView mainTextView;
-
- @Override
- protected void onCreate(Bundle savedInstanceState) {
- super.onCreate(savedInstanceState);
- setContentView(R.layout.activity_main);

-
- // 1. Access the TextView defined in layout XML
- // and then set its text
- mainTextView = (TextView) findViewById(R.id.main_textview);
- mainTextView.setText("Set in Java!");
- }
-
- @Override
- public boolean onCreateOptionsMenu(Menu menu) {
-
- // Inflate the menu; this adds items to the action bar if it is present.
- getMenuInflater().inflate(R.menu.menu_main, menu);
- return true;
- }
- }

Lastly, run your app again and look at what you have done.

You should see the text set via Java and, as a recap, this is what you did to make that happen like that:

- You added a new attribute to the **View** in XML – the ID attribute
- You used that new attribute to get into the **view** through your code
- You called a method on **View** so that you could change the value of the text.

Chapter 13 - Buttons and Listeners

Now it is time to do some work on building up **TextView** and making things a little more interactive. To do that, we are going to add **Button** in to you **activity_main.xml** file, straight after **TextView:**

- <!-- Set OnClickListener to trigger results when pressed -->
- <Button
- android:id="@+id/main_button"
- android:layout_width="wrap_content"
- android:layout_height="wrap_content"
- android:layout_marginTop="20dp"
- android:layout_marginLeft="20dp"
- android:text="@string/button" />

Did you spot the XML comment above the Button? This is a reminder on how to trigger results.

Look at the **layout_margin** attributes – they have added in 20 density independent (dp) pixels of space to the left and above the **Button** so that the layout doesn't appear overloaded and cramped. Remember, that value of 20 will be scaled by the density of the screen on whichever device it is on.

You may also have noticed **@string/button** has appeared in red underneath the button text property. Hover your mouse over the red and you will see that this is because there is a symbol that cannot be resolved – the reason for that is because we haven't defined it yet. To do that, open up **strings.xml** and add in this line at the bottom:

- <string name="button">Update The TextView</string>

Now open up **MainActivity.java** and ad in the following line, underneath the last line you added to put a variable in for the **TextView:**

- Button mainButton;

The line of code below needs to be added to the end of **onCreate**, right after the code that you added in before:

- // 2. Access the Button defined in layout XML
- // and listen for it here
- mainButton = (Button) findViewById(R.id.main_button);
- mainButton.setOnClickListener(this);

Once again, you did the same three steps as you did when you added in the code to gain access to **TextView:**

- You added the id attribute to **View** in XML, r, this time, you added in a view that has an id attribute
- That **View** can be accessed in code with the id attribute
- You can call methods on the **View**

This time, the method you have called is **setOnClickListener.** Now, this raises a question as to what object will respond when the button is pressed and the answer lies in whatever you put inside the parentheses of the method. To answer the question, all you need to do is add in **this,** which although it may seem somewhat unspecific, is correct because Java knows that **this** means that your intended listener is **MainActivity** and this means that **MainActivity** must implement the interface for **View.onClickListener.**

Now, Android Studio is pretty smart and will help you with the implementation. All you do is click on **this**, which you will see underlined in red – this indicates there is an error, which, in his case, is that **MainActivity** doesn't yet support the interface. When you see a red light bulb at the start of the line, click it and choose **Make 'MainActivity' implement 'android.view.View.onClickListener.**

Now click on OK on the next screen and Studio will generate the code you need to make **MainActivity** qualify as a certified **onClickListener.**

First of all, we added the following to the class declaration, thus indicating that **Activity** is to implement a specific interface:

- public class MainActivity extends ActionBarActivity implements View.OnClickListener
-

Secondly, Studio added in a stub for a method that has to be implemented to get the license for the **onClickListener** – the method is called **onClick** and will fire when that **Button** is pressed.

- @Override
- public void onClick(View v) {
-
- }

At the moment, the method does not do anything so we need to add in this code to **onClick** so it actually does something:

- // Test the Button
- mainTextView.setText("Button pressed!");

Now the app will change the text that is in **TextView** when the **Button** is pressed.

Chapter 14 - Adding Visual and Nested Layouts

It is always nice to see some pictures in an app interface so we are going to add in an **ImageView** so that we can get a small icon to show up. You will also see how the nested **LinearLayout** works.

First of all though, what image are you going to have displayed? The easiest way to start is with the image you got given as default. It's already there in your project and waiting to be used. All you have to do is find it. Use the Project Navigator and expand the directory called **res/drawable**

As you can see, there is a folder that contains a number of copies of the same image in **res.** All the file names have what looks like screen density abbreviations in brackets at the end. Those abbreviations do indeed relate to the pixel density buckets that are used to classify Android devise in dpi, or dots per inch.

- **mdpi:** medium
- **hdpi:** high
- **xhdpi:** extra high
- **xxhdpi:** extra extra high

Take a look inside the **drawable** directories and you should see a file called **ic_launcher.png.** This is the default launch image in a number of different sizes for different screens. The system will make sure the right one is picked for the device.

Head back to **activity_main.xml** and replace this section:

- <!-- Set OnClickListener to trigger results when pressed -->
- <Button
- android:id="@+id/main_button"
- android:layout_width="wrap_content"
- android:layout_height="wrap_content"
- android:layout_marginTop="20dp"
- android:layout_marginLeft="20dp"
- android:text="@string/button" />

With this:

- <!-- This nested layout contains views of its own -->
- <LinearLayout
- android:layout_width="wrap_content"
- android:layout_height="wrap_content"
- android:orientation="horizontal">
- <!-- Set OnClickListener to trigger results when

pressed -->
- `<Button`
- `android:id="@+id/main_button"`
- `android:layout_width="wrap_content"`
- `android:layout_height="wrap_content"`
- `android:layout_marginTop="20dp"`
- `android:layout_marginLeft="20dp"`
- `android:text="@string/button" />`
- `<!-- Shows an image from your drawable resources -->`
- `<ImageView`
- `android:layout_width="wrap_content"`
- `android:layout_height="wrap_content"`
- `android:layout_marginTop="20dp"`
- `android:layout_marginLeft="20dp"`
- `android:src="@drawable/ic_launcher" />`
- `<!-- Closing tag for the horizontal nested layout -->`
- `</LinearLayout>`

What you have done here is add a **LinearLayout** inside the root **LinearLayout** tool that already exists, directly under the **TextView** as its new sibling. You have also shifted the **Button** to the new nested layout and added in a new **ImageView**.

What you have achieved, by putting your **Button** inside another horizontal **LinearLayout** is the ability to put a **Button** and an **ImageView** horizontally side by side, even though the root layout is a vertical orientation.

The important attribute in **ImageView** is **src**, which is what you give your drawable image resource to. Note the format that you have used to reference the drawable image. Your image file name (without the file type) must be prefixed with **'drawable/'.**

Now run the app on your device or emulator again and you will see the image appear.

Chapter 15 - Involving the Keyboard

What about adding in some user input? We do this by introducing an **EditText** to the mix. This is a subclass of **TextView** that will display the keyboard and shows what the user is typing as content.

We are going to add **EditText** XML t **activity_main.xml** – it will be a sibling of **TextView** and **LinearLayout** (the horizontal one). Do watch that you don't catch it inside the nested layout though. You need to add it in after the closing of the embedded linear layout and before the closing of the root linear layout:

- <!-- Displays keyboard when touched -->
- <EditText
- android:id="@+id/main_edittext"
- android:layout_width="wrap_content"
- android:layout_height="wrap_content"
- android:layout_marginTop="20dp"

- android:layout_marginLeft="20dp"
- android:hint="@string/hint" />

We added a new special attribute in here – **hint.** This is a placeholder in the input field and it will be overwritten by the app as soon as the user begins typing. As per usual, you must define the string resource for the hint in **res/values.string.xml.**

- <string name="hint">A Name</string>

Open up **MainActivity.java** and add in a new variable for **EditText** (underneath the other two existing variables in the file).

- EditText mainEditText;

Now put the following code at the end of **onCreate**

- // 3. Access the EditText defined in layout XML
- mainEditText = (EditText) findViewById(R.id.main_edittext);

This code, in much the same way as the previous code, receives a reference to **EditText** control and saves it in the variable that has been assigned.

Now we have the reference to **EditText** control, it's time to do something with the user input. We are going to replace the contents of **onClick** with this:

- // Take what was typed into the EditText
- // and use in TextView
- mainTextView.setText(mainEditText.getText().toString()
- + " is learning Android development!");

Now, when **MainButton** is clicked, the **mainTextView** will display a string of test that includes the contents of **mainEditText** together with "**is learning Android Development!**"

Run your app and see what happens.

You should be getting user input with an **EditText,** submitted with a **Button** and displayed in a **TextView.**

Chapter 16 - The ListView

This is a very useful control that shows a lot of items visually. A **ListView** is defined the same way as any other view in XML. We are going to add a **ListView** as a sibling to **TextView, LinearLayout** horizontal and **EditText** in **activity_main.xml** by adding in the following code after the code for **EditText** control:

- <!-- List whose dataset is defined in code with an adapter -->
- <ListView
- android:id="@+id/main_listview"
- android:layout_width="match_parent"
- android:layout_height="0dp"
- android:layout_weight="1"
- android:layout_marginTop="20dp"/>

Just hold on a minute! How could it possibly work, setting **layout_height** to 0dp? It does not matter what device you are using, how big or small the screen is, 0dp can only scale to 0dp.

Now have a look at what comes after it. We have a **layout_weight** and, because nothing else in the layout has been given a weight just yet, the **ListView** will expand out to fill up as much space as it can, regardless of the value you have given l**ayout_height.**

So as a rule, the practice is to use a value of 0 so that the layout inflator doesn't have to think about a new dimension and the whole job gets done quicker.

Now. Open up **MainActivity.java** and add the following code variables underneath the ones that you added in the **onCreate** method:

- ListView mainListView;
- ArrayAdapter mArrayAdapter;
- ArrayList mNameList = new ArrayList();
-

The **ListView** variable makes perfect sense but what are the others all about? They are, t put it simply, to supply **ListView** with the data it will display. Bear with me on that one; first, I want you to add this code to end of **onCreate:**

- // 4. Access the ListView

- mainListView = (ListView) findViewById(R.id.main_listview);
-
- // Create an ArrayAdapter for the ListView
- mArrayAdapter = new ArrayAdapter(this,
- android.R.layout.simple_list_item_1,
- mNameList);
-
- // Set the ListView to use the ArrayAdapter
- mainListView.setAdapter(mArrayAdapter);

Some of this should look familiar by now because you are going to be finding **ListView** by using its id. But something else is going on here.

mArrayAdaptor is a go between so that **ListView** can get hold of the data that it needs. When you create this adaptor, you must specify the **Context** or the target XML view for the data – **simple_list_item_1** - and the data source, which is **mNameList.** But let's just back up a minute Do you remember writing any code that had an id of **simple_list_item_1?** Where did that come from? And just what is a **Context?**

Have a look at **android.R.layout** just before **simple_list_item_1.** There are a number of very important concepts in here but let's break this down and look at **R** first. This is a dynamically created class that will allow you access to the resources that are in your project. The R class can be used to get a resource ID and to do that you specify a resource name and type. The type would be somewhere along the lines of **string, drawable** or **layout** and this would be a match to the resource types in your project. And, as such, the **layout** bit in **android.R.layout.simple_list_item_1** specifies that you are referencing a layout resource, nothing more, nothing less.

But what about the **android** prefix? Why has that appeared? That is purely an indicator that it wasn't you who created that view and that it is a part of the Android platform, merely representing a **TextView** that any default list cell can draw on and use.

Context is an object that is representing the state of your app at the current time. If you need to access a particular service for use in your app then **context** is the one for you. It is used to create the views that are residing in your **ListView**. Cast your mind back to the layout resource you referred to – this is what the Context will take and convert to a view and the adapter simply populates the views with a value that it takes from its data source.

In this case, the data source is **mNameList**, which is nothing more than a list of strings. It is empty but it has been initialized so we need to add in a bit of data that **ListView** can display. Add in this code to the end of **onClick:**

- // Also add that value to the list shown in the ListView
- mNameList.add(mainEditText.getText().toString());

- mArrayAdapter.notifyDataSetChanged();

All you do is add in whatever was typed by the user into **EditText** to the names list and then push out a signal to the adaptor that it can update what is shown in **ListView.**

Now you can run your app again.

You should be able to type in a name to **EditText** and then see it shown in **TextView** as well as being added into a new row in **ListView** when you press the **Button.**

Chapter 17 - Detecting List Selections

Ok, so it's great to be able to look at the items in a list but you want some interactivity in your app. So, now we are going to set up a way for your app to detect user selections from that list. First, we have to make a modification to the class definition in **MainActivity.java** in order to add in some support for another interface. This line has to be modified:

- public class MainActivity extends ActionBarActivity implements View.OnClickListener {
-

To look like this:

- public class MainActivity extends ActionBarActivity implements View.OnClickListener, AdapterView.OnItemClickListener {
-

So, all you have done is add in support for the new interface, called **AdapterView.OnItemClickListener.** What this does, as the name tells you, is listens for selections of items from **ListView.**

You should also see a red line that is highlighting the line you just added your interface into. This is just Android Studio telling you that you have not actually implemented the interface just yet. This is easily fixed – click the highlighted line, press on **Alt+Enter**, click on **Implement Method** and then click **OK.**

Your next job is to ad in this line of code to the endo of **onCreate:**

- // 5. Set this activity to react to list items being pressed
- mainListView.setOnItemClickListener(this);

This code is setting **MainActivity** to listen for item clicks that occur on **mainListView.** So, now you need to replace **onItemClick** method, the one that was generated by default for you, with this code:

- @Override
- public void onItemClick(AdapterView<?> parent,

```
    View view, int position, long id) {

•
•    // Log the item's position and contents
•    // to the console in Debug
•    Log.d("omg    android",    position    +    ":    "    +
     mNameList.get(position));
•    }
```

Congratulations! You have set your **MainActivity** class to implement **onItemClick** so it can live up to its well-earned name as an **onItemClickListener.**

What is going on inside of **onItemClick** though? There is a strange **Log.d** showing up and there is something that has a **get (position)** in there as well.

Have a closer look at what you are passing to **onItemClick.** Specifically, look at **int position**. This is an integer that is equal to the index of the item that the user clicked on the list – integers count up from 0.

What has happened here is that you have taken the position and the index item from your names list and you have logged them. Logging is pretty basic but it is a very useful technique for debugging.

Run your app on your device or emulator, input a couple of values and then add them to your list. Now select any item – note that you do not see any visible effect at this point. Keep the app running but look at the section at the bottom of

Android Studio. This section holds information about the device or the emulator you are running, which processes and logs of what is going on in the processes. These logs show up in a console named **logcat.** It will reel off loads of information from your emulator or device and, to be honest, most of it is irrelevant to you at this stage. The log statements that you generated earlier are in here somewhere but there is a bit too much going on to see where they are.

To filter things out a bit, so you can see only what you want to see, look for an option at the top of the screen called **Log Level**. When you input the **Log** command into the code, you specified t as **Log.d**. The **d** stands for "debug" level – the other levels are:

- **V** - Verbose
- **D** - Debug
- **I** - Info
- **W** - Warning
- **E** - Error

When you choose a specific log level for **logcat** it shows only the messages that relate to that level or higher. Verbose is the lowest level, with Error being the highest. So, if you selected the Warning level, you will see only those for Warnings and for Errors.

In the meantime, you can also use the text box, which is at the right of the log level drop down menu, to pop in a filter and show the messages that contain just the text that you typed in. So, you can now set the level to **Debug** and type in the text box **omg android.**

You should now see a list of statements that relate to that and you will be able to see exactly when an item is picked from your list.

Chapter 18 - The Action Bar

Now your app has a number of different views so it's time to start thinking about how else you can add in functionality. On the older Android devices, there was a Menu device button that would show a load of options, depending on what the situation was, but since 2011, when Honeycomb was released, the Action Bar is used to display the items for the current view.

The Action bar is familiar, a good base for your users and, because it is present across apps, using this bar makes good sense in terms of the functionality of your app. On the flip side, if you opted not to use it, you could end up confusing a lot of users who would expect to see it working.

The Action Bar is already there in your app there just aren't any options attached just yet so that is the first thing we are going to look at doing.

Sharing

Very soon, using your own app, you will be able to show off the fact that you are learning Android development and you are going to do this by using an intersection of the **Intent** concept and the Action Bar – this is known as the **ShareActionProvider.**

An **Intent** has a number of advantages, one of which is the ability for you to be able to construct it in an **explicit** or **implicit** manner. When you defined the **Intent** that allows your app to launch, you used an example of the **explicit** type. The manifest identifies that as **MainActivity.** Now we are going to look at the **implicit** type and this is where a generic **Intention** is really going to come into play.

You see, some people want to share everything they do with everyone and others with just the select few. Instead of wondering which social network is a favorite of a particular user, and then integrating them one by one, you can tell the device that you want to share some content, expressing an **Intent**, and Android will do the rest.

Go to **res/menu/menu_main.xml** and open it. You will see some XML that has been automatically generated but it isn't needed. As such, you can replace the entire thing with this code:

- <!-- Defines the menu item that will appear on the Action Bar in MainActivity -->
- <menu xmlns:android="http://schemas.android.com/apk/res/android"
- xmlns:omgandroid="http://schemas.android.com/apk/res-auto">
- <!-- Share item -->
- <item
- android:id="@+id/menu_item_share"
- android:title="Share"
- omgandroid:showAsAction="ifRoom"
- omgandroid:actionProviderClass= "android.support.v7.widget.ShareActionProvider" />
- </menu>

Your app is going to be running on lower versions of Android than Lollipop so, quite often, you will need to use features that will not exist on these older versions. This means that you have to either build your own functionality to make sure your users enjoy a seamless experience across a range of different devices or you use third party libraries to provide it. Google has a number of **App Compatibility** libraries that you can use to try to cut down on this fragmentation problem.

In the above XML note that you are using **android.support.v7** libraries. Sing the support library means that the code you are going to implement will work on Android v7 and above.

Go to **MainActivity.java** and add in this variable under the variable you added last time:

- ShareActionProvider mShareActionProvider;

Now you should add in these two methods to class. The first is **onCreateOptionsMenu** and it may already have been implemented. If that is the case, just replace the implementation with this one:

- @Override
- public boolean onCreateOptionsMenu(Menu menu) {
-
- // Inflate the menu.
- // Adds items to the action bar if it is present.
- getMenuInflater().inflate(R.menu.menu_main, menu);
-
- // Access the Share Item defined in menu XML
- MenuItem shareItem = menu.findItem(R.id.menu_item_share);
-
- // Access the object responsible for
- // putting together the sharing submenu
- if (shareItem != null) {
- mShareActionProvider = (ShareActionProvider) MenuItemCompat.getActionProvider(shareItem);
- }
-
- // Create an Intent to share your content

- setShareIntent();
-
- return true;
- }
-
- private void setShareIntent() {
-
- if (mShareActionProvider != null) {
-
- // create an Intent with the contents of the TextView
- Intent shareIntent = new Intent(Intent.ACTION_SEND);
- shareIntent.setType("text/plain");
- shareIntent.putExtra(Intent.EXTRA_SUBJECT, "Android Development");
- shareIntent.putExtra(Intent.EXTRA_TEXT, mainTextView.getText());
-
- // Make sure the provider knows
- // it should work with that Intent
- mShareActionProvider.setShareIntent(shareIntent);
- }
- }

One important note here – if you see an implementation of **onOptionsItemsSelcted** in the class, you must take it out.

Add in your import that the **Activity** recognizes them. **onCreateOptionsMenu** will be called once when that activity is first started.

In a similar way to how you specified the layout XML file for the activity in **onCreate**, you now need to direct the menu inflator so that it looks at **menu_main.xml** to look for the items that need to go on the Action Bar.

Now you can access the menu item that you previously defined in XML by using its id, which is **menu_item_share** and you can then gain access to the action provider. Earlier, you specified that the action provider for this item was a **ShareActionProvider.** Because of that, you can safely cast to the type in the code and hold on to a reference via the **mShareActionProvider** variable.

The next step is to call **setShareIntent**. This is going to create an **Intent** but not just any old one. It will create and **Intent** that has an action you set to **ACTION SEND**. This is a generic action and simply tells Android that you want to send something. From here, you should set the content type of the **Intent** as subject, which is commonly used by email programs, and Text. The text will match whatever is showing in **TextView.**

Once everything has been done, you can pair **Intent** with **mShareActionProvider.** The code will work but only sort of. As it is, **setShareIntent** is only called once, at the creation of the menu. It would be so much better if we could have the **Intent** update every time the **TextView** changed; otherwise, that initial message will be there forevermore. To do that, add this code to the end of **onClick:**

- // 6. The text you'd like to share has changed,
- // and you need to update
- setShareIntent();

What you have done here is ensure that the share intent is always current.

Run the app and test out the sharing feature. Tap on the share icon on Action Bar and see if it shows up a range of choices, depending entirely on what your emulator or device has installed on it.

The **ShareActionProvider** will automatically pull up a range of possible share avenues based on the apps installed on the current device. If you are using an emulator, expect there to be less options whereas you may already have things like Facebook and Twitter installed on your device.

Chapter 19 - Remembering Your Name

So far everything that you have done, relating to user input, will only persist when the app is running. But what happens in between sessions? Now we want to add in some data persistence, with a brand new feature that is going to remember your name whenever you log in by recording it.

There are a few options in Android doe this but the easiest one to use is called **SharedPreferences.** This stores the data in key value pairs, which means that you specify the name, which is the key, for a specific piece of data, which is the value. When you save it, you can then retrieve it by using the original key. Let's see how this works.

First, you need to add in these constants and the variable to **MainActivity.java.** We will do this where the last variables were placed.

- private static final String PREFS = "prefs";

- private static final String PREF_NAME = "name";
- SharedPreferences mSharedPreferences;

This now puts **PREF** and **PREF NAME** right to the top of the class. **PREF** will be used as a file name so that you can keep your **SharedPreferences** in one place. **PREF NAME** will be used to store your name in shared preferences.

The last line adds in a variable called **mSharedPreferences** for the purpose of storing a particular reference to the shared preference class. You will only need access to this in a few places but hang on to it anyway. Add in the import to the class if you haven't already done so and then add these lines to the end of **onCreate:**

- // 7. Greet the user, or ask for their name if new
- displayWelcome();

This new code is calling the method **displayWelcome** so you can implement that by putting this method at the end of the class:

- public void displayWelcome() {
-
- // Access the device's key-value storage
- mSharedPreferences = getSharedPreferences(PREFS, MODE_PRIVATE);
-

- // Read the user's name,
- // or an empty string if nothing found
- String name = mSharedPreferences.getString(PREF_NAME, "");
-
- if (name.length() > 0) {
-
- // If the name is valid, display a Toast welcoming them
- Toast.makeText(this, "Welcome back, " + name + "!", Toast.LENGTH_LONG).show();
- }
- }

With this new method, the first thing you are doing is accessing **SharedPreferences** by using **MODE PRIVATE.** This means that the only app that can access the data that is stored here is your **OMG Android** app. This also means that the data you have saved cannot be overwritten by any other application that could have used the exact same key.

Next, you as the preferences object for the value that has been stored using key **PREF NAME.** The second parameter may be used to set up a default value that is returned in the case that there is no value stored with that key. In this case, you can use an empty **string** as the value.

Lastly, you need to check that the string has content and, if it does, it should display an output. Your message is going to be **Toast**, which will pop up and then fade away. **Toast** should be given a message that is can display and you should specify a built-in length of time to stay on the screen. Then just tell it to **show**. That's all there is to that.

Displaying the Name Dialog

What you have so far will show your name only if the app can get it from the preferences. However, that is little use to you at the moment because you haven't put anything in place to allow you to save your name.

To do that, we need a **Dialog**, which is a small window that will alert the user. They may have choices for the user to make. In this case, we are going to use an **AlertDialog.**

Add in this code to the end of **displayWelcome**, which is going to create an **else** branch for the existing **if** condition:

- } else {
-
- // otherwise, show a dialog to ask for their name
- AlertDialog.Builder alert = new AlertDialog.Builder(this);
- alert.setTitle("Hello!");
- alert.setMessage("What is your name?");
-
- // Create EditText for entry
- final EditText input = new EditText(this);

```
alert.setView(input);

// Make an "OK" button to save the name
alert.setPositiveButton("OK", new
DialogInterface.OnClickListener() {

public void onClick(DialogInterface dialog, int
whichButton) {

// Grab the EditText's input
String inputName = input.getText().toString();

// Put it into memory (don't forget to commit!)
SharedPreferences.Editor          e          =
mSharedPreferences.edit();
e.putString(PREF_NAME, inputName);
e.commit();

// Welcome the new user
Toast.makeText(getApplicationContext(),   "Welcome,
" + inputName + "!", Toast.LENGTH_LONG).show();
}
});

// Make a "Cancel" button
// that simply dismisses the alert
alert.setNegativeButton("Cancel", new
DialogInterface.OnClickListener() {

public void onClick(DialogInterface dialog, int
whichButton) {}
});
```

-
- alert.show();
- }

The app will reach the **else** condition only if there isn't a name that is valid, saved using the **PREF NAME** key. You will use an **AlertDialog.uilder** to provide a title, a message and an **EditText** to the **AlertDialog.** You will then add in a positive and a negative button to **AlertDialog.** First, you must define the text that is going to be shown on the buttons – use "OK" and "Cancel" for the sake of simplicity and second, you must define an **OnClickListener** for each button.

On this occasion, your **OnClickListeners** are going to be **DialogInterface.OnClickListeners** and you will define them straight away. The parameters for **OnClick** are a little different. On the positive button, **OnClick** is responsible for quite a bit. First, it will read the name that has been typed into **EditText** by the user. It will then save that name to **SharedPreferences** by way of a helper called a **SharedPreferencesEditor**. All you have to do is tell the editor what it needs to save and where it should save it, tell it to commit those changes and that is it.

Lastly, it will display a **Toast** that is the same as the other Welcoming one.

The negative button is somewhat simpler because it doesn't have to do anything.

Run your app and check out what's going on. You should be able to type in your name, press on OK and see the greeting. From here on in, that app will now remember your name and you will be personally greeted every time you open it.

Chapter 20: Android: How to Develop a Simple Calculator

Here, in this tutorial we will be developing an android calculator. For your better understanding, we will stick with the basic calculator. We use the android studio for developing this application.

Step 1:

Create a new android application project with the name of the project as "Calculator". Give the name "com.javahelps.calculator" as the name of the application.

Step 2:

By default, android will be using a green robot icon. You can use custom application icons for your projects and for using them, you should first delete the ic_launcher icon. This icon will be in the folder named mipmap. For all the applications, this is the launcher by default.

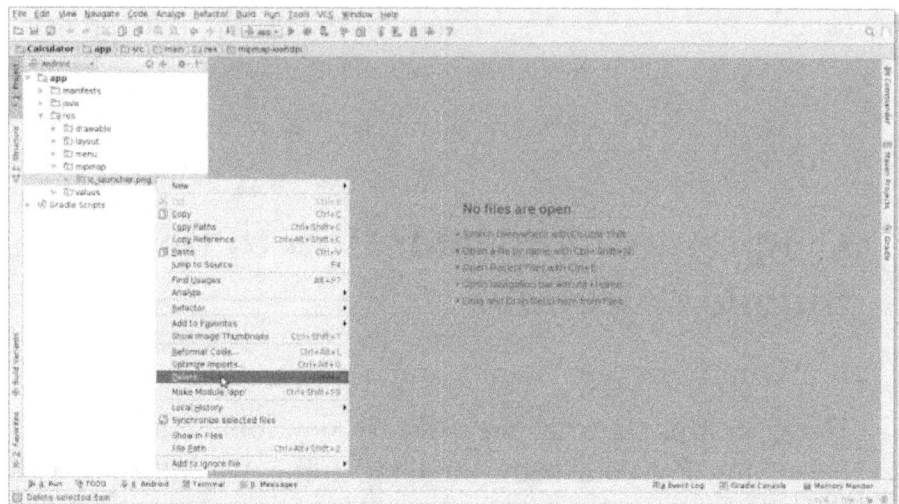

Step 3:

A PNG image file can be used as icon for the application. It is advised that you use a file with a minimum pixel size of 256x256. This selected image will be set as the application icon in the Google play store and in the application.

Step 4:

Right click on the "mipmap" folder and select New and Image Asset from New.

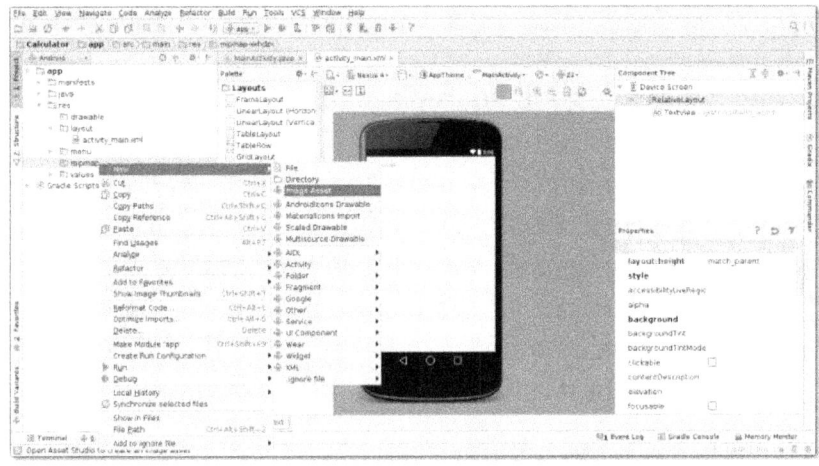

Step 5:

Browse for your icon from your computer and select the file. Click on the Next and Finish buttons. Ensure that the name of the resource is ic_launcher before selecting Next and Finish.

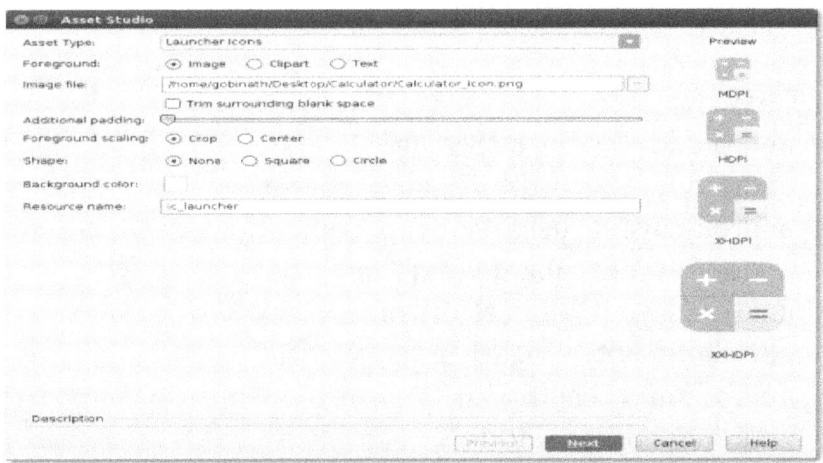

Step 6:

Use the following code to replace the content in the file activity_main.xml. A TextView will be created by this code for the necessary buttons and the number screen of the calculator. For preventing the manual user input with the android a default keypad, we will use the TextView in place of the EditText. Not all of the common properties are given in this code. You should make sure that the given four attributes for the buttons are included in your code.

```
android:layout_width="0dp"
android:layout_height="match_parent"
android:layout_weight="1"
android:textSize="30sp"

<RelativeLayout
xmlns:android="http://schemas.android.com/apk/res/android"
  xmlns:tools="http://schemas.android.com/tools"
  android:layout_width="match_parent"
  android:layout_height="match_parent"
  tools:context=".MainActivity">

  <TextView
    android:id="@+id/txtScreen"
    android:layout_width="match_parent"
    android:layout_height="wrap_content"
    android:layout_alignParentTop="true"
    android:layout_centerHorizontal="true"
    android:gravity="right|center_vertical"
    android:maxLength="16"
    android:padding="10dp"
    android:textAppearance="?android:attr/textAppearance
Large"
```

```xml
        android:textSize="30sp"
        android:typeface="serif"                                    />

    <LinearLayout
        android:layout_width="match_parent"
        android:layout_height="match_parent"
        android:layout_below="@+id/txtScreen"
        android:orientation="vertical">

        <LinearLayout
            android:layout_width="match_parent"
            android:layout_height="0dp"
            android:layout_weight="1">
            <Button
                android:id="@+id/btnSeven"
                android:text="7" />

<Button
            android:id="@+id/btnEight"
            android:text="8"                                    />
            <Button
                android:id="@+id/btnNine"
                android:text="9"/>
            <Button
                android:id="@+id/btnDivide"
                android:text="/"/>
        </LinearLayout>

        <LinearLayout
            android:layout_width="match_parent"
            android:layout_height="0dp"
            android:layout_weight="1">
            <Button
                android:id="@+id/btnFour"
```

```xml
        android:text="4"/>
    <Button
      android:id="@+id/btnFive"
      android:text="5"                                    />
    <Button
      android:id="@+id/btnSix"
      android:text="6"                                    />
    <Button
      android:id="@+id/btnMultiply"
      android:text="*"                                    />
</LinearLayout>

<LinearLayout
    android:layout_width="match_parent"
    android:layout_height="0dp"
    android:layout_weight="1">
    <Button
      android:id="@+id/btnOne"
      android:text="1"                                    />
    <Button
      android:id="@+id/btnTwo"
      android:text="2"                                    />
    <Button
      android:id="@+id/btnThree"
      android:text="3"                                    />
    <Button
      android:id="@+id/btnSubtract"
      android:text="-"                                    />
</LinearLayout>

<LinearLayout
    android:layout_width="match_parent"
    android:layout_height="0dp"
    android:layout_weight="1">
```

```
<Button
    android:id="@+id/btnDot"
    android:text="."                            />
<Button
    android:id="@+id/btnZero"
    android:text="0"                            />
<Button
    android:id="@+id/btnClear"
    android:text="C"                            />
<Button
    android:id="@+id/btnAdd"
    android:text="+"                            />
    </LinearLayout>

    <Button
    android:id="@+id/btnEqual"
    android:text="="                            />
  </LinearLayout>
</RelativeLayout>
```

Step 7:

Select New by right clicking on the folder "drawable" and then select Drawable resource file.

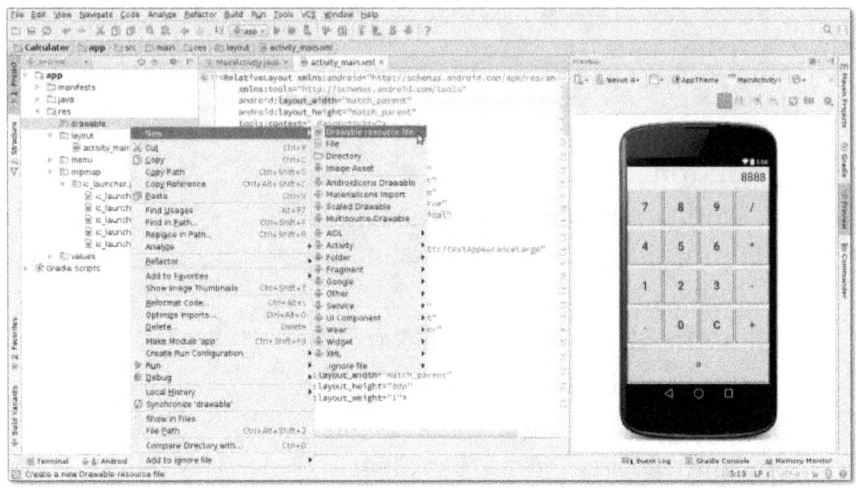

Step 8:

Now create a drawable file and name it as "button".

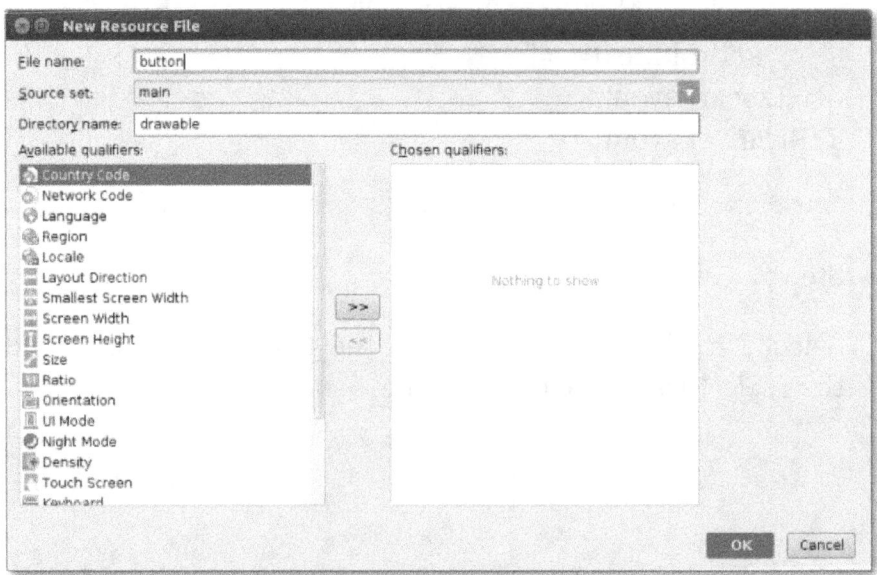

Step 9:

Now, use the following code for replacing the button.xml file's content. For decorating the calculator buttons, this drawable resource will be used. In this code, two gradient shapes are given. One gradient shape is used for the normal state of the button and the second gradient shape is used for the button pressed state.

```xml
<?xml version="1.0" encoding="utf-8" ?>
<selector
xmlns:android="http://schemas.android.com/apk/res/android">
  <item android:state_pressed="true">
    <shape>
      <gradient android:angle="90"
android:endColor="#FFFFFF"
android:startColor="#9EB8FF" android:type="linear" />
      <padding android:bottom="0dp" android:left="0dp"
android:right="0dp" android:top="0dp" />
      <size android:width="60dp" android:height="60dp"
/>
      <stroke android:width="1dp"
android:color="#ff3da6ef" />
    </shape>
  </item>
  <item>
    <shape>
      <gradient android:angle="90"
android:endColor="#FFFFFF"
android:startColor="#ffd9d9d9" android:type="linear" />
      <padding android:bottom="0dp" android:left="0dp"
android:right="0dp" android:top="0dp" />
      <size android:width="60dp" android:height="60dp"
/>
```

```
        <stroke android:width="0.5dp"
android:color="#ffcecece" />
    </shape>
  </item>
</selector>
```

Step 10:

Add the property "android:background" to all of the activity_main.xml buttons.

```
android:background="@drawable/button"
```

Step 11:

The library exp4J is used to evaluate the arithmetic expressions in this project. From the Gradle scripts, select the file "build.gradle (Module: app)". A dependency 'net.objecthunter:exp4j:0.4.4' will now be added to the project. It is shown in the code given below.

```
dependencies {
  compile fileTree(dir
: 'libs', include: ['*.jar'])
  compile 'com.android.support:appcompat-v7:21.0.3'
  compile 'net.objecthunter:exp4j:0.4.4'
}
```

You will be asked to sync the project by the android studio after saving your file. Click on the link present on the top left corner for syncing your project. For downloading the Gradle libraries, you should be connected to the Internet.

Step 12:

From the provided code, modify the MainActivity.java. The description for the code is added in the comments.

package com.javahelps.calculator;
import android.os.Bundle;
import android.support.v7.app.ActionBarActivity;
import android.view.View;
import android.widget.Button;
import android.widget.TextView;

import net.objecthunter.exp4j.Expression;
import net.objecthunter.exp4j.ExpressionBuilder;

public class MainActivity extends ActionBarActivity {
    // IDs of all the numeric buttons
    private int[] numericButtons = {R.id.btnZero, R.id.btnOne,

```java
R.id.btnTwo, R.id.btnThree, R.id.btnFour, R.id.btnFive,
R.id.btnSix, R.id.btnSeven, R.id.btnEight, R.id.btnNine};
    // IDs of all the operator buttons
    private int[] operatorButtons = {R.id.btnAdd,
R.id.btnSubtract, R.id.btnMultiply, R.id.btnDivide};
    // TextView used to display the output
    private TextView txtScreen;
    // Represent whether the lastly pressed key is numeric or
not
    private boolean lastNumeric;
    // Represent that current state is in error or not
    private boolean stateError;
    // If true, do not allow to add another DOT
    private boolean lastDot;

    @Override
    protected void onCreate(Bundle savedInstanceState) {
        super.onCreate(savedInstanceState);
        setContentView(R.layout.activity_main);
        // Find the TextView
        this.txtScreen = (TextView)
findViewById(R.id.txtScreen);
        // Find and set OnClickListener to numeric buttons
        setNumericOnClickListener();
        // Find and set OnClickListener to operator buttons,
equal button and decimal point button
        setOperatorOnClickListener();
    }

    /**
     * Find and set OnClickListener to numeric buttons.
     */
    private void setNumericOnClickListener() {
        // Create a common OnClickListener
```

```java
        View.OnClickListener listener = new
View.OnClickListener() {
            @Override
            public void onClick(View v) {
                // Just append/set the text of clicked button
                Button button = (Button) v;
                if (stateError) {
                    // If current state is Error, replace the error
message
                    txtScreen.setText(button.getText());
                    stateError = false;
                } else {
                    // If not, already there is a valid expression so
append to it
                    txtScreen.append(button.getText());
                }
                // Set the flag
                lastNumeric = true;
            }
        };
        // Assign the listener to all the numeric buttons
        for (int id : numericButtons) {
            findViewById(id).setOnClickListener(listener);
        }
    }

    /**
     * Find and set OnClickListener to operator buttons, equal
button and decimal point button.
     */
    private void setOperatorOnClickListener() {
        // Create a common OnClickListener for operators
        View.OnClickListener listener = new
View.OnClickListener() {
```

```java
        @Override
        public void onClick(View v) {
            // If the current state is Error do not append the
operator
            // If the last input is number only, append the
operator
            if (lastNumeric && !stateError) {
                Button button = (Button) v;
                txtScreen.append(button.getText());
                lastNumeric = false;
                lastDot = false;   // Reset the DOT flag
            }
        }
    };
    // Assign the listener to all the operator buttons
    for (int id : operatorButtons) {
        findViewById(id).setOnClickListener(listener);
    }
    // Decimal point
    findViewById(R.id.btnDot).setOnClickListener(new
View.OnClickListener() {
        @Override
        public void onClick(View v) {
            if (lastNumeric && !stateError && !lastDot) {
                txtScreen.append(".");
                lastNumeric = false;
                lastDot = true;
            }
        }
    });
    // Clear button
    findViewById(R.id.btnClear).setOnClickListener(new
View.OnClickListener() {
        @Override
```

```java
    public void onClick(View v) {
        txtScreen.setText("");  // Clear the screen
        // Reset all the states and flags
        lastNumeric = false;
        stateError = false;
        lastDot = false;
    }
});
// Equal button
findViewById(R.id.btnEqual).setOnClickListener(new
View.OnClickListener() {
    @Override
    public void onClick(View v) {
        onEqual();
    }
});
}

/**
 * Logic to calculate the solution.
 */
private void onEqual() {
    // If the current state is error, nothing to do.
    // If the last input is a number only, solution can be
found.
    if (lastNumeric && !stateError) {
        // Read the expression
        String txt = txtScreen.getText().toString();
        // Create an Expression (A class from exp4j library)
        Expression expression = new
ExpressionBuilder(txt).build();
        try {
            // Calculate the result and display
            double result = expression.evaluate();
```

```
            txtScreen.setText(Double.toString(result));
            lastDot = true; // Result contains a dot
        } catch (ArithmeticException ex) {
            // Display an error message
            txtScreen.setText("Error");
            stateError = true;
            lastNumeric = false;
        }
    }
}
}
```

Step 13:

Run the application after saving the changes.

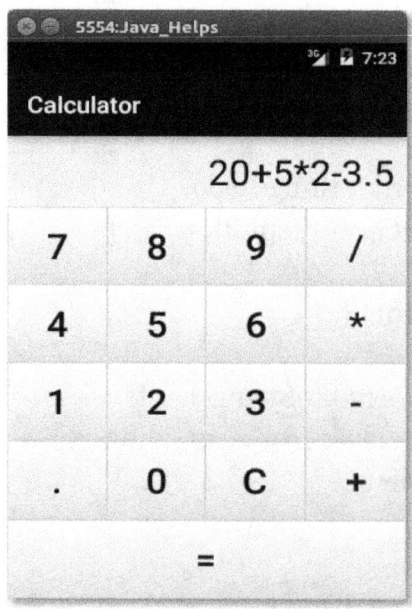

Chapter 21: Android: A login Application

A login application is nothing but a screen that asked for your login credentials for logging into application. You must be familiar with such login applications from social websites like Twitter, Facebook, etc,.

This chapter will explain you how a login screen is created and how the security is managed in case of false attempts.

Two TextViews should be defined asking for the user's username and password. The TextView of the password must have its inputType on password. The syntax for them is given below.

Syntax

```
<EditText
  android:id="@+id/editText2"
  android:layout_width="wrap_content"
  android:layout_height="wrap_content"
  android:inputType="textPassword" />
```

```
<EditText
 android:id="@+id/editText1"
 android:layout_width="wrap_content"
 android:layout_height="wrap_content"
/>
```

A button should be defined with login text and its property should be set to onClick. After this, the function mentioned below should be defined in the Java file's onClick property.

```
<Button
 android:id="@+id/button1"
 android:layout_width="wrap_content"
 android:layout_height="wrap_content"
 android:onClick="login"
 android:text="@string/Login"
/>
```

Get The text of the username and password inside the onClick method of the Java file by using the methods getText() and toString(). Now by using the equals() function, match the text.

```
EditText username =
(EditText)findViewById(R.id.editText1);
EditText password =
(EditText)findViewById(R.id.editText2);
public void login(View view){
  if(username.getText().toString().equals("admin") &&
password.getText().toString().equals("admin")){

  //correct password
```

```
}else{
//wrong password
}
```

Now, for the last thing, you should provide a security mechanism for preventing unwanted attempts. For this, you should initialize available and it should be decrement with each false attempt. The login button should be disabled when the count reaches zero.

```
int counter = 3;
counter--;
if(counter==0){
//this will disable the button and closes the application

}
```

Example

An example is given below demonstrating a login application. This will create a basic application and it will only give you 3 attempts for logging in.

You can use this code on an emulator are on an actual device to test it.

Steps   Description

1   For creating an android application we will use the
         android   studio   and   the   package
         com.example.sairamkrishna.myapplication. You should
         make sure that you are getting the software development

	kit and you should compile it with the most recent version of the SDK while creating the project, so that you can use the APIs of higher level.
3	For adding the necessary code, modify the file src/MainActivity.java
4	For adding the respective XML components, modify the file res/layout/activity_main
5	You can run the application by installing it on a running android device and can verify the results.

The file modified is src/MainActivity.java. The modified main activity file's content is given below.

```
package com.example.sairamkrishna.myapplication;

import android.app.Activity;
import android.graphics.Color;
import android.os.Bundle;

import android.view.Menu;
import android.view.MenuItem;
import android.view.View;

import android.webkit.WebView;
import android.webkit.WebViewClient;

import android.widget.Button;
import android.widget.EditText;
import android.widget.TextView;
```

```java
import android.widget.Toast;

import java.io.FileInputStream;
import java.io.FileOutputStream;

public class MainActivity extends Activity  {
  Button b1,b2;
  EditText ed1,ed2;

  TextView tx1;
  int counter = 3;

  @Override
  protected void onCreate(Bundle savedInstanceState) {
    super.onCreate(savedInstanceState);
    setContentView(R.layout.activity_main);


b1=(Button)findViewById(R
.id.button);
    ed1=(EditText)findViewById(R.id.editText);
    ed2=(EditText)findViewById(R.id.editText2);


b2=(Button)findViewById(R
.id.button2);
    tx1=(TextView)findViewById(R.id.textView3);
    tx1.setVisibility(View.GONE);

    b1.setOnClickListener(new View.OnClickListener() {
      @Override
      public void onClick(View v) {
        if(ed1.getText().toString().equals("admin") &&
```

```java
                ed2.getText().toString().equals("admin")) {
                    Toast.makeText(getApplicationContext(),
"Redirecting...",Toast.LENGTH_SHORT).show();
                }
                else{
                    Toast.makeText(getApplicationContext(), "Wrong
Credentials",Toast.LENGTH_SHORT).show();

                    tx1.setVisibility(View.VISIBLE);
                    tx1.setBackgroundColor(Color.RED);
                    counter--;
                    tx1.setText(Integer.toString(counter));

                    if (counter == 0) {
                        b1.setEnabled(false);
                    }
                }
            }
        });

    b2.setOnClickListener(new View.OnClickListener() {
        @Override
        public void onClick(View v) {
            finish();
        }
    });
}


@
Override
 public boolean onCreateOptionsMenu(Menu menu) {
    // Inflate the menu
;
this adds items to the action bar if it is present
```

```
        getMenuInflater().inflate(R.menu.menu_main, menu);
        return true;
    }

    @
Override
    public boolean onOptionsItemSelected(MenuItem item) {
        // Handle action bar item clicks here
. The action bar will
        //
automatically handle clicks on the Home/Up button, so long
        // as you specify a parent activity in AndroidManifest
.xml.

        int id = item.getItemId();

        //
noinspection SimplifiableIfStatement
        if (id == R.id.action_settings) {
            return true
;
        }
        return super.onOptionsItemSelected(item);
    }
}
```

res/layout/activity_main.xml is the modified XML file and
its content is given below.

```
<RelativeLayout
xmlns:android="http://schemas.android.com/apk/res/andr
oid"
```

```
  xmlns:tools="http://schemas.android.com/tools"
android:layout_width="match_parent"
  android:layout_height="match_parent"
android:paddingLeft="@
dimen/activity_horizontal_margin
"
  android:paddingRight="@dimen/activity_horizontal_marg
in"
  android:paddingTop="@
dimen/activity_vertical_margin
"
  android:paddingBottom="@dimen/activity_vertical_margi
n" tools:context=".MainActivity">

  <TextView android:text="Login"
android:layout_width="wrap_content"
    android:layout_height="wrap_content"
    android:id="@+id/textview"
    android:textSize="35dp"
    android:layout_alignParentTop="true"
    android:layout_centerHorizontal="true" />

  <TextView
    android:layout_width="wrap_content"
    android:layout_height="wrap_content"
    android:text="welcome"
    android:id="@+id/textView"
    android:layout_below="@+id/textview"
    android:layout_centerHorizontal="true"
    android:textColor="#ff7aff24"
    android:textSize="35dp" />

  <EditText
    android:layout_width="wrap_content"
```

```
    android:layout_height="wrap_content"
    android:id="@+id/editText"
    android:hint="Enter Name"
    android:focusable="true"
    android:textColorHighlight="#ff7eff15"
    android:textColorHint="#ffff25e6"
    android:layout_marginTop="46dp"
    android:layout_below="@+id/imageView"
    android:layout_alignParentLeft="true"
    android:layout_alignParentStart="true"
    android:layout_alignParentRight="true"
    android:layout_alignParentEnd="true" />

<ImageView
    android:layout_width="wrap_content"
    android:layout_height="wrap_content"
    android:id="@+id/imageView"
    android:src="@drawable/abc"
    android:layout_below="@+id/textView"
    android:layout_centerHorizontal="true" />

<EditText
    android:layout_width="wrap_content"
    android:layout_height="wrap_content"
    android:inputType="textPassword"
    android:ems="10"
    android:id="@+id/editText2"
    android:layout_below="@+id/editText"
    android:layout_alignParentLeft="true"
    android:layout_alignParentStart="true"
    android:layout_alignRight="@+id/editText"
    android:layout_alignEnd="@+id/editText"
    android:textColorHint="#ffff299f"
    android:hint="Password" />
```

```
<TextView
  android:layout_width="wrap_content"
  android:layout_height="wrap_content"
  android:text="Attempts Left:"
  android:id="@+id/textView2"
  android:layout_below="@+id/editText2"
  android:layout_alignParentLeft="true"
  android:layout_alignParentStart="true"
  android:textSize="25dp" />

<TextView
  android:layout_width="wrap_content"
  android:layout_height="wrap_content"
  android:text="New Text"
  android:id="@+id/textView3"
  android:layout_alignTop="@+id/textView2"
  android:layout_alignParentRight="true"
  android:layout_alignParentEnd="true"
  android:layout_alignBottom="@+id/textView2"
  android:layout_toEndOf="@+id/textview"
  android:textSize="25dp"
  android:layout_toRightOf="@+id/textview" />

<Button
  android:layout_width="wrap_content"
  android:layout_height="wrap_content"
  android:text="login"
  android:id="@+id/button"
  android:layout_alignParentBottom="true"
  android:layout_toLeftOf="@+id/textview"
  android:layout_toStartOf="@+id/textview" />

<Button
```

```
    android:layout_width="wrap_content"
    android:layout_height="wrap_content"
    android:text="Cancel"
    android:id="@+id/button2"
    android:layout_alignParentBottom="true"
    android:layout_toRightOf="@+id/textview"
    android:layout_toEndOf="@+id/textview" />

</RelativeLayout>
```

The res/values/string.xml file's content is given below.

```
<resources>
  <string name="app_name">My Application</string>
  <string name="hello_world">Hello world!</string>
  <string name="action_settings">Settings</string>
</resources>
```

The AndroidManifest.xml file's content is given below.

```
<?xml version="1.0" encoding="utf-8"?>
<manifest
xmlns:android="http://schemas.android.com/apk/res/andr
oid"
  package="com.example.sairamkrishna.myapplication" >

  <uses-permission
android:name="android.permission.INTERNET" />

  <application
    android:allowBackup="true"
    android:icon="@mipmap/ic_launcher"
    android:label="@string/app_name"
    android:theme="@style/AppTheme" >
```

```xml
    <activity
      android:name=".MainActivity"
      android:label="@string/app_name" >

      <intent-filter>
        <action android:name="android.intent.action.MAIN"
/>
        <category
android:name="android.intent.category.LAUNCHER" />
      </intent-filter>

    </activity>

  </application>
```

Chapter 22: Android Animations

Using animations

From the android version 3.0, the properties animation API is introduced. Over the predefined time interval, this allowed the change of the object properties.

The arbitrary properties to an object can be defined using the API. This attribute can be given a start value and end value. Time based changes can also be given to this attribute.

1.2. Animator and AnimatorListener

The Animator class is the superclass of the animation API. For modifying the object's attributes, the ObjectAnimator class is typically used.

An AnimatorListener class can also be added to your Animator class. During different phases of the animation this listener will be called. This listener can be used for performing actions after or before an animation. For example, it can be used for adding or removing a View from a certain ViewGroup.

1.3. ViewPropertyAnimator

From the android version 3.1, the ViewPropertyAnimator was introduced. This class provides simpler access to the animations that are performed on views.

A ViewPropertyAnimator will be returned by the animate() method. Simultaneous animations are allowed to perform by this object. It allows you to set the duration of animation and it has got a fluent API.

The ViewPropertyAnimator is designed with the main purpose of providing a simpler API for typical animations.

This method's usage is shown in the example given below.

```
// Using hardware layer
myView.animate().translationX(400).withLayer();
```

By allowing the ViewPropertyAnimator use the hardware layout, the performance can be optimised.

```
// Using hardware layer
myView.animate().translationX(400).withLayer();
```

A runnable can be directly defined for executing it during the beginning and ending of the animation.

```
// StartAction
myView.animate().translationX(100).withStartAction(new
Runnable(){
 public void run(){
  viewer.setTranslationX(100-myView.getWidth());
  // do something
 }
});
```

```
// EndAction
myView.animate().alpha(0).withStartAction(new
Runnable(){
 public void run(){
   // rRemove the view from the parent layout
   parent.removeView(myView);
 }
});
```

You can define objects of the type TimeInterpolator using the setInterpolator(). The TimeInterpolator is used for defining the value changed over time. It is a linear standard. There are a few default ones defined by the android platform. The rate of change for them is slow at the start and the end but it accelerates in the middle.

The objects of the TypeEvaluator type can we set using the setEvaluator method. With the TypeEvaluator, animations can be created on arbitrary property types. Custom evaluators should be provided for the ones that cannot be understood and used automatically by the animation system.

Layout animations

On a layout container, you can set animations using the LayoutTransition class. The container's change on the view hierarchy will be animated.

```
package com.example.android.layoutanimation;

import android.animation.LayoutTransition;
import android.app.Activity;
```

```java
import android.os.Bundle;
import android.view.Menu;
import android.view.View;
import android.view.ViewGroup;
import android.widget.Button;


public class MainActivity extends Activity {

 private
ViewGroup viewGroup;

 @Override
 public void onCreate(Bundle savedInstanceState) {
   super.onCreate(savedInstanceState);
   setContentView(R.layout.activity_main);
   LayoutTransition l = new LayoutTransition();
   l.enableTransitionType(LayoutTransition.CHANGING);
   viewGroup = (ViewGroup) findViewById(R.id.container);
   viewGroup.setLayoutTransition(l);

 }


public void onClick(View view
) {
   viewGroup.addView(new Button(this));
 }

 @Override
 public boolean onCreateOptionsMenu(Menu menu) {
   getMenuInflater().inflate(R.menu.activity_main, menu);
   return true;
 }
```

}

Animations for Activity transition

We all know that the animations can be applied on views. But it is not limited to them. Animations can be applied on transition between activities too.

The customer or default animations can be defined using the ActivityOptions class.

```
public void onClick(View view) {
 Intent intent = new Intent(this
, SecondActivity.class);
 ActivityOptions options =
ActivityOptions.makeScaleUpAnimation(view, 0,
    0, view.getWidth(), view.getHeight());
 startActivity(intent, options.toBundle());
}
```

View Animation

The below description is given that you already have some basic knowledge on android development.

In this tutorial will look at the properties of the animation API and its usage.

Now, create a new project and name it com.vogella.android.animation.views and the activity AnimationExampleActivity. The default layout file will be the main.xml. You should change that file to be given code.

```xml
<?xml version="1.0" encoding="utf-8"?>
<RelativeLayout
xmlns:android="http://schemas.android.com/apk/res/android"
  android:id="@+id/layout"
  android:layout_width="match_parent"
  android:layout_height="match_parent"
  android:orientation="vertical" >

  <LinearLayout
    android:id="@+id/test"
    android:layout_width="wrap_content"
    android:layout_height="wrap_content" >

    <Button
      android:id="@+id/Button01"
      android:layout_width="wrap_content"
      android:layout_height="wrap_content"
      android:onClick="startAnimation"
      android:text="Rotate" />

    <Button
      android:id="@+id/Button04"
      android:layout_width="wrap_content"
      android:layout_height="wrap_content"
      android:onClick="startAnimation"
      android:text="Group" >
    </Button>

    <Button
      android:id="@+id/Button03"
      android:layout_width="wrap_content"
      android:layout_height="wrap_content"
      android:onClick="startAnimation"
```

```
      android:text="Fade" />

   <Button
      android:id="@+id/Button02"
      android:layout_width="wrap_content"
      android:layout_height="wrap_content"
      android:onClick="startAnimation"
      android:text="Animate" />

  </LinearLayout>

  <ImageView
      android:id="@+id/imageView1"
      android:layout_width="wrap_content"
      android:layout_height="wrap_content"
      android:layout_centerHorizontal="true"
      android:layout_centerVertical="true"
      android:src="@drawable/icon" />

  <TextView
      android:id="@+id/textView1"
      android:layout_width="wrap_content"
      android:layout_height="wrap_content"
      android:layout_above="@+id/imageView1"
      android:layout_alignRight="@+id/imageView1"
      android:layout_marginBottom="30dp"
      android:text="Large Text"
      android:textAppearance="?android:attr/textAppearance
Large" />

</RelativeLayout>
```

Create the following menu resource.

```
<?xml version="1.0" encoding="utf-8"?>
```

```xml
<menu
xmlns:android="http://schemas.android.com/apk/res/android" >

  <item
    android:id="@+id/item1"
    android:showAsAction="ifRoom"
    android:title="Game">
  </item>

</menu>
```

Change your activity to the following.

```java
package com.vogella.android.animation.views;

import android.animation.AnimatorSet;
import android.animation.ObjectAnimator;
import android.app.Activity;
import android.content.Intent;
import android.graphics.Paint;
import android.os.Bundle;
import android.view.Menu;
import android.view.MenuItem;
import android.view.View;
import android.widget.ImageView;
import android.widget.TextView;

public class AnimationExampleActivity
extends Activity {


/** Called when the activity is first created. */
```

```java
@Override
public void onCreate(Bundle savedInstanceState) {
  super.onCreate(savedInstanceState);
  setContentView(R.layout.main);

}

public void startAnimation(View view) {
  float dest = 0;
  ImageView aniView = (ImageView)
findViewById(R.id.imageView1);
  switch (view.getId()) {

  case R.id.Button01:
    dest = 360;
    if (aniView.getRotation() == 360) {
      System.out.println(aniView.getAlpha());
      dest = 0;
    }
    ObjectAnimator animation1 =
ObjectAnimator.ofFloat(aniView,
        "rotation", dest);
    animation1.setDuration(2000);
    animation1.start();
    // Show how to load an animation from XML
    // Animation animation1 =
AnimationUtils.loadAnimation(this,
    // R.anim.myanimation);
    // animation1.setAnimationListener(this);
    // animatedView1.startAnimation(animation1);
    break;

  case R.id.Button02:
```

```
// shows how to define a animation via code
// also use an Interpolator (BounceInterpolator)
Paint paint = new Paint();
TextView aniTextView = (TextView)
findViewById(R.id.textView1);
float measureTextCenter =
paint.measureText(aniTextView.getText()
    .toString());
dest = 0 - measureTextCenter;
if (aniTextView.getX() < 0) {
  dest = 0;
}
ObjectAnimator animation2 =
ObjectAnimator.ofFloat(aniTextView,
    "x", dest);
animation2.setDuration(2000);
animation2.start();
break;

case R.id.Button03:
// demonstrate fading and adding an AnimationListener

dest = 1;
if (aniView.getAlpha() > 0) {
  dest = 0;
}
ObjectAnimator animation3 =
ObjectAnimator.ofFloat(aniView,
    "alpha", dest);
animation3.setDuration(2000);
animation3.start();
break;

case R.id.Button04:
```

```java
    ObjectAnimator fadeOut =
ObjectAnimator.ofFloat(aniView, "alpha",
    0f);
    fadeOut.setDuration(2000);
    ObjectAnimator mover =
ObjectAnimator.ofFloat(aniView,
    "translationX", -500f, 0f);
    mover.setDuration(2000);
    ObjectAnimator fadeIn =
ObjectAnimator.ofFloat(aniView, "alpha",
    0f, 1f);
    fadeIn.setDuration(2000);
    AnimatorSet animatorSet = new AnimatorSet();

    animatorSet.play(mover).with(fadeIn).after(fadeOut);
    animatorSet.start();
    break;

  default:
    break;
  }

}

@Override
public boolean onCreateOptionsMenu(Menu menu) {
  getMenuInflater().inflate(R.menu.mymenu, menu);
  return super.onCreateOptionsMenu(menu);
}

@Override
public boolean onOptionsItemSelected(MenuItem item) {
  Intent intent = new Intent(this, HitActivity.class);
```

```
    startActivity(intent);
    return true;
  }
}
```

Create a new activity called HitActivity.

```
package com.vogella.android.animation.views;

import java.util.Random;

import android.animation.Animator;
import android.animation.AnimatorListenerAdapter;
import android.animation.AnimatorSet;
import android.animation.ObjectAnimator;
import android.app.Activity;
import android.os.Bundle;
import android.view.View;
import android.widget.Button;

public class HitActivity extends Activity {
 private ObjectAnimator animation1;
 private ObjectAnimator animation2;
 private Button button;
 private Random randon;
 private int width;
 private int height;
 private AnimatorSet set;

 @Override
 protected void onCreate(Bundle savedInstanceState) {
   super.onCreate(savedInstanceState);
   setContentView(R.layout.target);
   width =
getWindowManager().getDefaultDisplay().getWidth();
```

```java
    height =
getWindowManager().getDefaultDisplay().getHeight();
    randon = new Random();

    set = createAnimation();
    set.start();
    set.addListener(new AnimatorListenerAdapter() {

      @Override
      public void onAnimationEnd(Animator animation) {
        int nextX = randon.nextInt(width);
        int nextY = randon.nextInt(height);
        animation1 = ObjectAnimator.ofFloat(button, "x",
button.getX(),
            nextX);
        animation1.setDuration(1400);
        animation2 = ObjectAnimator.ofFloat(button, "y",
button.getY(),
            nextY);
        animation2.setDuration(1400);
        set.playTogether(animation1, animation2);
        set.start();
      }
    });
    }

  public void onClick(View view) {
    String string = button.getText().toString();
    int hitTarget = Integer.valueOf(string) + 1;
    button.setText(String.valueOf(hitTarget));
  }

  private AnimatorSet createAnimation() {
    int nextX = randon.nextInt(width);
```

```
  int nextY = randon.nextInt(height);

button = (Button) findViewById(R
.id.button1);
  animation1 = ObjectAnimator.ofFloat(button, "x", nextX);
  animation1.setDuration(1400);
  animation2 = ObjectAnimator.ofFloat(button, "y", nextY);
  animation2.setDuration(1400);
  AnimatorSet set = new AnimatorSet();
  set.playTogether(animation1, animation2);
  return set;
 }
}
```

By pressing different buttons after running this example, the animation will be started. You can navigate to the other activity using the ActionBar.

Animations for fragment transitions

Animations can be defined during fragment transactions and they should be used to basing on the Animation API property through the method setCustomAnimations().

Android provides many standard animations and you can use those are using the method call setTransition(). The FragmentTransaction.TRANSIT_FRAGMENT_* constraints are used for a defining them.

You can define entry and exit animations using any of the two methods.

Activity animations in Android with shared views

Animations can be done between activities from the android version 5.0. Between these activities they can have shared views. If shared part is defined, the old you will start animating into the size and position of the new one.

You can create a top-level package project for testing it. calledcom.vogella.android.activityanimationwithsharedview s.

Create two activities with different layouts. Both of them should contain the same android:transitionNameproperty in the ImageView

activity_main.xml

```
<LinearLayout
xmlns:android="http://schemas.android.com/apk/res/andr
oid"
  xmlns:tools="http://schemas.android.com/tools"
  android:layout_width="match_parent"
  android:layout_height="match_parent"
  android:paddingBottom="@dimen/activity_vertical_marg
in"
  android:paddingLeft="@dimen/activity_horizontal_margi
n"
  android:paddingRight="@dimen/activity_horizontal_mar
gin"
  android:paddingTop="@dimen/activity_vertical_margin"
  tools:context=".MainActivity">

  <ImageView
    android:id="@+id/sharedimage"
    android:layout_width="match_parent"
    android:layout_height="wrap_content"
```

```
    android:scaleType="centerCrop"
    android:src="@drawable/ic_sharedimage"
    />

</LinearLayout>
```

activity_second.xml

```
<RelativeLayout
xmlns:android="http://schemas.android.com/apk/res/andr
oid"
  xmlns:tools="http://schemas.android.com/tools"
  android:layout_width="match_parent"
  android:layout_height="match_parent"
  android:paddingBottom="@dimen/activity_vertical_marg
in"
  android:paddingLeft="@dimen/activity_horizontal_margi
n"
  android:paddingRight="@dimen/activity_horizontal_mar
gin"
  android:paddingTop="@dimen/activity_vertical_margin"
  tools:context="com.vogella.android.activityanimationwiths
haredviews.SecondActivity">

  <ImageView
    android:id="@+id/sharedimage"
    android:layout_width="match_parent"
    android:layout_height="wrap_content"
    android:src="@drawable/ic_sharedimage"
    android:layout_alignParentBottom="true"
    android:layout_alignParentEnd="true" />

  <TextView
    android:layout_width="wrap_content"
    android:layout_height="wrap_content"
```

```xml
        android:text="@string/hello_world"
        android:id="@+id/textView" />

    <Button
        android:layout_width="wrap_content"
        android:layout_height="wrap_content"
        android:text="New Button"
        android:id="@+id/button"
        android:transitionName="sharedImage"
        android:layout_below="@+id/textView"
        android:layout_alignParentStart="true"
        android:layout_marginTop="54dp" />

</RelativeLayout>
```

Adjust your activity code.

```java
package
com.vogella.android.activityanimationwithsharedviews;

import android.app.Activity;
import android.app.ActivityOptions;
import android.content.Intent;
import android.os.Bundle;
import android.view.View;
import android.widget.ImageView;


public class MainActivity extends Activity {

    @Override
    protected void onCreate(Bundle savedInstanceState) {
        super
.onCreate(savedInstanceState);
        setContentView(R.layout.activity_main);
```

```java
    final ImageView sharedImage = (ImageView)
findViewById(R.id.sharedimage);
    sharedImage.setOnClickListener(new View.
OnClickListener() {
        @Override
        public void onClick(View view
) {

            //This is where the magic happens.
            // makeSceneTransitionAnimation takes a context,
view,
            // a name for the target view.
            ActivityOptions options =
                ActivityOptions.
                makeSceneTransitionAnimation(MainActivity.this,
sharedImage, "sharedImage");

Intent intent = new Intent(MainActivity
.this, SecondActivity.class);
            startActivity(intent, options.toBundle());
        }
    });

  }

}

package
com.vogella.android.activityanimationwithsharedviews;

import android.app.Activity;
import android.os.Bundle;


public class SecondActivity extends Activity
```

```
{

    @Override
    protected void onCreate(Bundle savedInstanceState) {
        super.onCreate(savedInstanceState);
        setContentView(R.layout.activity_second);
    }
}
```

After running the application, if you click on the image view, it will be animated with the same property android:transitionName and it is the button in this case.

Conclusion

There you have it, a simple Android app that you can develop yourself and astound your friends with. There is so much further you can go with this but that is getting into more advanced waters.

Keep on practicing and you will soon be in a position to advance on to more complex coding and writing deeper programs that do more. Don't just practice your Android development though; go back to the roots and make sure you keep up to date with your Java language as well because this is an important part of the development process.

Good luck and don't forget to have fun!

You May Enjoy My Other Books!

PYTHON: Programming Guide For Beginners: LEARN IN A DAY!

hyperurl.co/python

C ++ Programming : Programming Language For Beginners: LEARN IN A DAY!

hyperurl.co/cplusplus

JAVA: Java Programming, JavaScript, Coding: Programming Guide: LEARN IN A DAY!

hyperurl.co/javaos

SQL: Programming Guide: Javascript and Coding: LEARN IN A DAY!

hyperurl.co/sql

Programming HTML: Programming Guide: Computer Programming: LEARN IN A DAY!

hyperurl.co/html

Programming Swift: Create A Fully Functioning App: Learn In A Day!

hyperurl.co/swift

www.ingramcontent.com/pod-product-compliance
Lightning Source LLC
Chambersburg PA
CBHW070949200526
45161CB00001BA/48